Thomas Hatfield
Bishop, Soldier, and Politician

Thomas Hatfield (c. 1310–81) rose from origins amongst the Yorkshire gentry to become a valued royal servant under King Edward III. As such, he participated in the elaborate administration required for warfare in France in the late 1330s. Clerical careers in royal administration could lead to ecclesiastical office through royal patronage, and Hatfield's qualities marked him for early promotion. In 1345 he was elected Bishop of Durham, an office he held until his death. As bishop he retained a strong connection with royal service. He was also employed in the management of northern England and England's relations with Scotland. At the same time, he remained a dedicated advocate of the autonomy of the Durham palatinate over which he ruled as bishop. Hatfield's long episcopacy ensured that he made his mark on his bishopric and on the cathedral church of Durham, where his elaborate tomb is still seen. Hatfield College, a college of Durham University, is named after him.

Based on a series of lectures given at Hatfield College in 2010, the assumed seven hundredth anniversary of Thomas Hatfield's birth, this volume highlights the unique military, political, and clerical roles he performed and his notable legacies. The studies in this volume advance knowledge of both the man and his remarkable career and, in so doing, enhance understanding of the wider secular and religious world in which he lived.

DURHAM PUBLICATIONS
IN MEDIEVAL AND RENAISSANCE STUDIES

Thomas Hatfield
Bishop, Soldier, and Politician

Lectures Given at Hatfield College, Durham University, in Honour of the Seven Hundredth Anniversary of the Birth of Bishop Thomas Hatfield

Edited by
ANTHONY BASH

Institute of Medieval and Renaissance Studies
Durham University

Pontifical Institute of Mediaeval Studies
Toronto

Library and Archives Canada Cataloguing in Publication

Thomas Hatfield : bishop, soldier, and politician / edited by Anthony Bash

Lectures given at Hatfield College, Durham University, in honour of the seven hundredth anniversary of the birth of Bishop Thomas Hatfield.
Durham publications in medieval and Renaissance studies.
Includes bibliographical references and index.
Co-published by: Institute of Medieval and Renaissance Studies, Durham University.

ISBN 978-0-88844-440-0

1. Hatfield, Thomas, 1310?–1381 – Congresses. 2. Hatfield, Thomas, 1310?–1381 – Military leadership – Congresses. 3. Catholic Church. Bishopric of Durham (England) – History – Congresses.
4. Catholic Church – Great Britain – Bishops – Biography – Congresses.
5. Durham (England : County) – Church history – Congresses.
6. Great Britain – History – Edward III, 1327–1377 – Congresses.
I. Bash, Anthony, 1952– II. Pontifical Institute of Mediaeval Studies
III. University of Durham. Institute of Medieval and Renaissance Studies

BX1495.D87 T56 2012 274.28/605 23 C2012-904865-8

Pontifical Institute of Mediaeval Studies
59 Queen's Park Crescent East
Toronto, Ontario, Canada M5S 2C4
www.pims.ca

MANUFACTURED IN CANADA

Contents

List of Illustrations

Plates appear following page 34

ANTHONY BASH

Preface

In 2010 Hatfield College celebrated the seven hundredth anniversary of the likely date of the birth of the bishop after whom the College is named, Thomas Hatfield.

Some of us at the College knew relatively little about Bishop Hatfield. Even the College archivist's *History* of the College has only one paragraph on Bishop Hatfield.[1] We felt it was time to learn more, as well as to celebrate our eponymous founder.

To that end, in Epiphany Term 2010, we held a lecture series at the College on Thomas Hatfield. Our thanks go to Richard Britnell for guiding us as to whom to approach to speak. We are grateful to Michael Prestwich, Mark Ormrod, Christian Liddy, and Richard Britnell for giving the lectures. Edited versions of the lectures appear in this book.

Later in the year, at evensong on the eve of Hatfield Day,[2] the Bishop of Durham, Dr N.T. Wright – himself a formidable New Testament scholar – gave an address on Bishop Hatfield, which is printed as Appendix One. Dr David Boardman, who attended the lectures in Epiphany Term, has contributed a second appendix on Durham Cathedral in Bishop Hatfield's time.

We now bring the lectures and the other contributions to a wider public. I am confident the lectures – in their quality, depth, and range of learning – aptly illustrate our College motto, *Vel primus vel cum primis*.

1 W.A. Moyes, *Hatfield 1846–1996: A History of Hatfield College in the University of Durham* (Durham: Hatfield College Trust, 1996), 3.

2 "Hatfield Day" is the College's annual celebration (held towards the end of Easter term) to mark the end of the University's examination period. The College commemorates Bishop Hatfield at choral evensong in Durham Cathedral the day before.

T.P. BURT

Introduction

As far as anyone can tell, Thomas Hatfield was born in 1310, so a series of lectures – the basis of this book – seemed most appropriate in 2010, his assumed seven hundredth anniversary. Those lectures were held in the College that bears his name, Hatfield College, Durham, and organized by the College Chaplain, the Rev Dr Anthony Bash, to whom we extend our grateful thanks. In addition to the four lectures reproduced here, this book includes a sermon given in the cathedral by Bishop Tom Wright on the eve of Hatfield Day 2010, a fitting culmination to the lecture series in many ways. We also have a second appendix by David Boardman describing the architecture of the cathedral in Hatfield's era.

The four chapters that follow have added a great deal to our knowledge of Thomas Hatfield. Some details remain unknown: not only exactly when he was born but where. Michael Prestwich argues that it was most likely Hatfield Magna in Holderness, but it may have been at Hatfield, north-east of Doncaster. Either way, his home region had already proven a fruitful source of highly talented royal clerks, and Thomas Hatfield was no exception. Once recruited, he rose rapidly through the ranks. As Mark Ormrod observes, his role as receiver of the chamber translates today as private secretary to the Queen, whilst as keeper of the privy seal, he was effectively the home secretary of his day. Both King Edward III and Thomas Hatfield held their roles for a long time, and they were clearly close friends by the time the old King died. As one of Edward's trusted advisers, Hatfield's appointment as Bishop of Durham was no surprise, even if his young age perturbed some people, including, perhaps, the Pope.

It is a complicated matter to review Hatfield's achievements, not least because of the relative lack of archival sources – though available sources are better than they might have been – and the huge contrast in the governance of the kingdom between then and now. Weighing up Hatfield's various roles as soldier, politician, and, of course, bishop is therefore a difficult task, and we are grateful to Michael Prestwich, Mark Ormrod, and Christian Liddy for their insights. There can be no doubt of Hatfield's importance. His participation as a soldier (in France) was notable, though his work as peacemaker and diplomat (with Scotland) contributed more to upholding the English kingdom. As Bishop of Durham he had more power within the palatinate than the King and exercised it when needed. Most significantly, he was an experienced administrator, trusted by the King. Notwithstanding, his first loyalty remained to his palatinate and to those who lived in this northern "tax haven." I have always been impressed by the length of his episcopacy (1345–81); it is obvious that he must have been an adept politician, well capable of reconciling the positions of servant of the King and servant of the church and self-evidently well capable of surviving in post over several decades. He may not have been pious, but the church was well served by him, and he was vigorous in his defence of the palatinate.

Richard Britnell surveys Hatfield's legacy, starting with the architecture of the bishop's throne in Durham Cathedral. He then moves on to matters of utmost significance to the College that bears his name: the crest and the motto. The Hatfield College crest is essentially Thomas Hatfield's, with a surrounding border of ermine to satisfy the College of Heralds.[1] Interestingly, we find that the College motto, *Vel primus vel cum primis*, is taken from the description of Hatfield in the *Continuation of the History of Durham*: "He always strove to be the first or amongst the first." Richard Britnell did not raise the question of why, at a late stage, Durham University changed its original choice of name for its new college in 1846 from St. Cuthbert's Hall to Hatfield Hall. Robin Widdison, Tutor at the College and former Senior Lecturer in the Department of Law, has speculated that this may have related to the date, 1846. Was the naming of Hatfield Hall in recognition of the five hundredth anniversary in 1845 of Hatfield's appointment as bishop in 1345? Or perhaps it was to commemorate his presumed role at the battle of Neville's Cross in 1346? If the latter, it was in hindsight not a good reason, now that Michael Prestwich has given firm evidence that Hatfield was not there at all!

Thomas Hatfield was prone to self-importance and had a high opinion of himself – but why not? He was, after all, in a unique position as Bishop of the Durham palatinate. Would we have liked him? Possibly

1 W.A. Moyes, *Hatfield 1846–1996: A History of Hatfield College in the University of Durham* (Durham: Hatfield College Trust, 1996).

not, but rather like Hatfield College, he was evidently untroubled by those who envied his position (and energetic in defending it). Can the College that bears his name be proud of him? Certainly. He was a notable and successful leader who made major and lasting contributions at local, regional, and national levels. Moreover, in financing what eventually became Trinity College, Oxford, he showed his support for university education even though he never enjoyed that privilege himself.

The choice of name for Hatfield Hall was, then, a good one. Thomas Hatfield was a most important figure in fourteenth-century England, well worthy of lasting recognition, and the chapters which follow provide an unprecedented insight into his life and legacy.

MICHAEL PRESTWICH

Thomas Hatfield at War

Bishop Thomas Hatfield's seal does not look like a bishop's seal. It is round, not oval, and on the reverse it shows him mounted, on a caparisoned horse, bearing a shield. His sword is sheathed; his helmet has a crest of a mitre, from which a plume of feathers rises. The mitre is the only indication on this side of the shield that we are dealing with a clergyman, not a knight, though of course the other side portrays Hatfield as a bishop, seated on a throne. The image of him mounted and equipped for war shows that he was a man with unusually martial ambitions for a bishop.

Hatfield probably came from Hatfield Magna in Holderness, but there still some uncertainty about his origins; the antiquary, George Poulson, who placed him there, gave his father's name as Walter, but other sources have listed it as John. However, Poulson showed the coat of arms for the Hatfields of Hatfield Magna was the one which Thomas Hatfield used, according to the Calais roll of arms. Another Hatfield, to the northeast of Doncaster, is a possible alternative birthplace; it is in the same region, not far from the Humber. A large number of royal clerks in the early fourteenth century came from East Yorkshire and North Lincolnshire. Along with Hatfield, Ferriby, Airmyn, and Wetwang are among the place names which were also surnames of clerks who served in the fourteenth-century royal household. William Melton, Archbishop of York from 1316 to 1340, a particularly notable royal clerk, came from near Hull.

Given the uncertainty over Hatfield's birthplace, his family background can only be guessed at. He was probably a member of the minor gentry; his brother William became a knight, but none of his ancestors appears to have been of this status, and there is no evidence to suggest that the family had a military tradition. There is no indication as to how Hatfield was educated; there is no record of his attending university and obtaining a degree. This was not unusual for a clerk in the King's service; for the most part, such men received their training on the job. Archbishop Melton was exceptional in having attended university at Oxford.

Recruitment into royal service was, no doubt, a matter of personal recommendation and patronage. It is very possible that Thomas Hatfield entered the royal household at an early age, with his career path set as a royal clerk from the outset, but there is no evidence of his being in royal service until 1337. In the summer of that year, he was listed as one of the twenty-nine royal chaplains. In August he was appointed the clerk in charge of paying wages to the workmen engaged in major building operations at Stirling Castle, and from October he had the same role at Bothwell. Edward III himself supervised the work at Bothwell, and Hatfield must have impressed him, for in June of the following year, in a remarkably rapid rise to an important post, he became receiver of the chamber.

The chamber was the section of the administration that was closest to the King. Unfortunately, remarkably few chamber records survive. This is particularly so for Hatfield's time, for once he presented his accounts at the end of his tenure of office, he took the unprecedented step of burning all his rolls and memoranda, so that he would be free of any possible charges that might be levied in the future. This was done with the King's consent. Hatfield remained receiver of the chamber until December 1344, by which time he was also keeper of the privy seal, an office he held until July 1345. In this position he would have been very close to the King, preparing all kinds of writs and instructions on Edward's behalf, though not formal charters and documents such as those issued by the royal chancery. How well Hatfield performed remains a matter of conjecture. One historian, T.F. Tout, rather unkindly described Hatfield, along with his colleague William Kilsby, as "admirably qualified by ability and lack of scruple" to carry out the work of government.[1] The fact that he had his records burned, and the evident value the King set upon him, suggests that there is some justification for such a verdict.

The posts he held put Hatfield at the heart of a government dedicated to war. In 1337 the great conflict with France, known at the Hundred Years War, started, and Hatfield as receiver of the chamber was soon heavily involved. The initial phase of the war saw little action; the King

1 T.F. Tout, *Chapters in the Administrative History of Mediaeval England: The Wardrobe, the Chamber and the Small Seals*, 6 vols. (1920–33; repr. Manchester and New York, 1967), 2: 87.

went with a small force to Flanders, where he had a jolly time, as one chronicler put it. The two armies, the English with their allies, and the French, faced each other in 1339, but departed without fighting a battle. The English ravaged territory in northern France, and in 1340 achieved an unexpected naval victory at Sluys. The war then petered out with the English government effectively bankrupt. The siege of Tournai by Edward III and his allies failed. A new phase began in 1341 with a disputed succession in Brittany; this came to an end with a truce in 1343. Meanwhile, English forces were holding their own in Gascony in southwestern France. Instead of going to reinforce them in 1346, Edward III landed his army in Normandy, and proceeded on an astonishing campaign which culminated in the victory at Crécy, and, in the following year, the capture of Calais.

As an important household clerk, Hatfield would have expected to take part in these campaigns. There were many precedents, particularly from Edward I's reign, when the leading clerks in the King's service went to war, mounted on splendid chargers, with substantial armed retinues. In 1298 John Benstead, controller of the wardrobe, had a force of 2 knights, 10 men-at-arms, and 3 clerks. This was a man who later gave up his clerical career, married, and became a knight. In 1300 John Droxford, keeper of the wardrobe, had a retinue of 6 knights and 22 squires. His was the largest force in the household, outnumbering even that of the steward, Walter Beauchamp, the man in charge of the household knights, whose following numbered 2 knights and 13 squires. Droxford did not follow Benstead's example by becoming a knight, but went on to be Bishop of Bath and Wells. Ralph Manton, cofferer of the wardrobe, went to war in Scotland in 1298 on a horse worth 50 marks, the sort of value to be expected for an earl's mount. He had the misfortune to be ambushed at Roslin in 1303, where he was killed. The Scottish force was led by Simon Fraser, a turncoat who had earlier served as one of Edward I's household knights. Fraser rebuked Manton for wearing armour rather than priestly robes, and also for not paying out wages properly.

It is therefore no surprise that Hatfield would have gone to war with his retinue. An entry in the wardrobe account book for 1338–40 notes that he took forty-four horses to Flanders, for himself and his men. The wages section of the accounts notes that Hatfield initially had three squires with him, but this number soon rose to thirteen. He was paid three shillings a day, the same rate as knights who were entitled to dine in the King's hall, though for a period of twenty-five days he received double wages. Hatfield was far from the grandest of the household clerks. William Kilsby, keeper of the privy seal, had a banneret, 2 knights, and 28 squires and men-at-arms in his company, with 102 horses, and William Norwell, keeper of the wardrobe, had 2 knights and 20 men-at-arms, with 70 horses. These two clerks were Hatfield's superiors, and it would have been inappropriate if he had a grander retinue than theirs.

Hatfield was soon promoted to the status of banneret. This was a purely military rank, above that of a knight. Its holders were entitled to bear a rectangular banner, rather than a triangular pennon. Accounts show that Hatfield served with 2 knights and 11 squires from 25 November 1341 to 13 January of the following year; he was also accompanied by sixteen hobelars, lightly armed horsemen. The record does not specify where the campaigning occurred, but Hatfield must surely have accompanied the King north to Scotland, where he wintered at Melrose. In August 1342 Hatfield went to Brittany, serving there until 15 February 1343, by which time a truce had been agreed upon. His force on this occasion consisted of 3 knights, 16 squires, and 20 archers.

It is not known whether Hatfield was actively engaged in fighting on these campaigns. As a cleric, he was formally prohibited by the law of the church from drawing blood, though there were theorists who allowed the clergy to fight in a just war. He was probably more preoccupied with the administration of war than with the cut and thrust of hand-to-hand conflict. The loss of his accounts has left him as a rather shadowy figure, but some of his activities are on record. Money was needed for the expeditionary force in Flanders, and in 1338 Hatfield took £5,000 from Norwich to Walton-on-the-Naze, using three carts and with an escort of ten archers. In 1339 he went on an important financial mission to Germany, visiting Trier and continuing on by boat to Cologne, taking some of the royal jewels with him to pledge against loans. He received a loan of 16,000 florins from the Italian merchant bankers, the Bardi and Peruzzi, and even pawned the King's great crown. There are intriguing hints that he may also have acted as a spymaster in the Low Countries. He paid £2 5s. to two German minstrels who brought news to the King, and £2 4s. to Alard de Lisle, who was sent on what must have been a very dangerous mission, to spy within the French court. He also paid a large sum, £67, to a German knight engaged on what was described as "secret business of the king." He bought a springald, a type of siege weapon, for the King's use.

In 1345 Hatfield's career in the royal household came to an end, when he became Bishop of Durham. This was a very normal career trajectory. In the decade 1345–55, each keeper of the privy seal became either an archbishop (John Thoresby and Simon Islip) or a bishop (Hatfield and Roger Northburgh). It might be expected that this elevation would mark the end of Hatfield's military role, but while most bishops did not fight, this was not to be the case. There was, however, a precedent, in the form of Antony Bek, the grandest of all Bishops of Durham, who while holding the see had become Patriarch of Jerusalem. He emphatically did not give up military aspirations when he became bishop. Bek commanded the division of the English army that took Dirleton Castle on Edward I's campaign in Scotland in 1298. Admittedly, Edward I had some doubts about the bishop, for when Bek initially failed to take the castle, he sent John FitzMarmaduke to ask the King for reinforcements. "Go back," said Edward, "and tell the bishop that he may be a pious man in his episcopal office, but he should exercise no piety in this business."[2]

More contemporary to Hatfield, there was the example of John Kirkby, Bishop of Carlisle, who in 1336 had contracted to fight in Scotland with a retinue of forty men-at-arms. Of greater significance was the Bishop of Lincoln, Henry Burghersh. He was described by a chronicler as "a man of great distinction, wise in counsel, urbanely bold, of outstanding powers, and a shrewd manager of fighting men."[3] Burghersh went on the expedition to Flanders at the start of the Hundred Years War, with 5 bannerets, 24 knights, and 75 squires as his retinue, which was certainly equal to that of an earl. He was approaching fifty, and whether he actually fought is not known, but it is unlikely, for no battle took place, and the main duties he undertook were diplomatic. However, he was on the 1339 campaign in the Thierache, in northern France, in which villages and lands were burned. In the next year, before the battle of Sluys, he went ashore with Reginald Cobham, persuaded the Flemings to join in the coming engagement, and observed the French navy.

2 *The Chronicle of Walter of Guisborough*, ed. Harry Rothwell, Camden series 89 (London, 1957), 325.

3 *Knighton's Chronicle, 1337–1396*, ed. and trans. G.H. Martin (Oxford, 1995), 27–9.

Burghersh was, however, exceptional. He was the only bishop in the English army in Flanders in the early stages of the French war. William Zouche, Archbishop of York, was present at the battle of Neville's Cross in 1346, but the circumstances were unusual, for the King and most of his magnates were away fighting in France. His successor Archbishop Thoresby, a former royal administrator like Hatfield, did not fight. A man such as Thomas Lisle, Bishop of Ely, considered by his biographer to have been the Al Capone of the bench of bishops, and whose followers were accused of "a host of crimes ranging from petty theft and extortion to kidnapping, arson, assault and murder,"[4] might be expected to have had military ambitions, but he, too, did not go to war.

Hatfield, of course, was not an ordinary bishop. There were doubts about his elevation to his see. Pope Clement VI is said to have declared, when he appointed Hatfield to the see of Durham, that he would promote a jackass if the King nominated one. Hatfield was described as *iuvenis*, a young man. He was in fact about thirty-five, but this was young for a bishop. A chronicler reported that the cardinals considered him *levis et laicus*, and so unsuitable. There was little reason for him to change his ways on his promotion, though, and every reason to continue to give Edward III his fullest support, which would mean going to war. In 1345, however, he stayed in England, for he was appointed as a councillor to the King's son Lionel, who was acting as regent during the King's absence abroad.

The great campaign in which Hatfield took part was that of 1346, which culminated in the battle of Crécy. In 1346 the English adopted a new strategy, when they invaded Normandy. It was thought that the purpose of the expedition was to go to Gascony, to relieve the siege of Aiguillon. It may be that the fleet was genuinely intended to go to Gascony, but that contrary winds forced a landing in Normandy. On the other hand, the Gascony plan may have been a clever deception. At all events, the fleet which sailed on 11 July landed at La Hougue a couple of days later. The landing was clearly unexpected, and the English met limited resistance.

There are good accounts of the expedition; there is a diary of sorts, which provides a day-to-day account of events, and a number of news-

4 John Aberth, *Criminal Churchmen in the Age of Edward III: The Case of Bishop Thomas de Lisle* (University Park, PA, 1996), xvii.

letters, sent home to announce the triumphs. The advance went remarkably well; the town of Caen was captured on 26 July. The plan was then to advance northwards; reinforcements were expected at Le Crotoy, near the mouth of the Somme. This, however, involved crossing the Seine, and the bridges were broken. The army marched along the river, getting closer and closer to Paris. Poissy was reached on 13 August, and though the bridge there was broken, it was repairable. It took three days before the army could cross, but cross it did. Meanwhile, Edward issued challenges to the French to come and fight; he even suggested single combat with the French king. According to the campaign diary, the King had appointed commanders for the army on 17 July. The Earl of Northampton was to be constable, and the Earl of Warwick marshal. The vanguard was under the Prince of Wales, the centre under the King, and the rearguard under Hatfield. With him were the Earls of Arundel, Suffolk, and Huntingdon, and a number of named lords, including James Audley. It was very unusual to appoint a bishop to such an important command in this way. It has been argued that during the Hundred Years War, command was increasingly professionalized, and instead of appointing men because of their high social status, the more sensible option of selecting men for their expertise was adopted. Men such as Thomas Dagworth and Walter Bentley were proving their worth in the war in Brittany. There were, however, problems in appointing men purely on merit. Robert Knollys was one of the great English soldiers of the Hundred Years War, but when he was appointed to command a force in 1370, he faced mutiny from the more aristocratic John Minsterworth. It would, however, be wrong to assume that earls were unprofessional; those who served Edward III were men with immense military experience. Four of them had been selected for promotion in 1337 from the ranks of household bannerets and knights, and there can be little doubt that military ability was one of the reasons for their elevation. In Hatfield's case, however, rank counted for more than experience. As a bishop, he outranked an earl. Purely in terms of precedence, it was appropriate to give him command. An alternative might have been to keep him close to the King; but given the fact that he did have military experience, the decision was a sensible one. The rearguard was not the best command. In 1364 at the battle of Auray, Sir Hugh Caveley was most upset at being appointed to the rearguard – was he not as good as the others? It took some persuasion from Sir John Chandos before he would accept the position.

What did Hatfield's role amount to in practice? He had three earls with him, and it is likely that they exercised command in practice, just as in the prince's battalion it would have been the Earls of Northampton and Warwick who would have done so. The newsletters from the campaign contain no mention of Hatfield, but they mention very few English names, and so it is no real reflection on Hatfield that he is not one of them. Regrettably, there is no evidence to show what he did during the march to Poissy. One historian has assumed that he said mass in the mornings, but it is more likely that he relied upon his chaplains to conduct services.

Hatfield had a very large retinue on this campaign. Unfortunately, for the Crécy expedition there are no surviving full pay rolls or valuation lists of horses (the latter were prepared so that men could be compensated should their mounts die or be killed). It is possible, however, to reconstruct Hatfield's following from other sources. A sixteenth-century summary of the wardrobe account book shows that his retinue consisted of 3 bannerets, 48 knights, 162 esquires, and 81 archers, a total of 294 men. This was on a par with most of the earls. Warwick had 348 men; Arundel, 304; Northampton, 302; Huntingdon, 224; and Suffolk, a mere 159. Admittedly, all these were dwarfed by those of the Earl of Lancaster with 1,376 men, and the Prince of Wales with 1,343. Even so, Hatfield's following was impressively large, particularly when compared with other clerics. Walter de Wetwang, keeper of the wardrobe, had 3 knights, 25 esquires, and 35 archers, and John Thoresby, Hatfield's successor as keeper of the privy seal, 2 knights, 30 esquires, and 36 archers. William Kilsby, who had devoted himself to a military career after losing his office of keeper of the privy seal in 1342, had a following of 3 knights, 73 esquires, and 79 archers.

The names of about forty of Hatfield's followers are known, for they were exempted from recruitment by other lords, and received letters of protection to ensure that legal action could not be brought against them when they were on campaign. There were few men from the palatinate of Durham among them. Hatfield had not been bishop for long, after all, and would have had his own connections that he probably considered much more reliable when it came to recruiting a retinue. For the most part Hatfield's following was drawn from the Midlands. Marmaduke and Thomas of Lumley were the only two from Durham; William de Felton was from Northumberland. John de Fauconberg was from Yorkshire, though his family was connected by marriage to the Nevilles of Durham.

More significantly, Walter de Fauconberg had shared the lordship of Hatfield Magna with Walter Hatfield.

Once the bridge at Poissy had been repaired, the English army made its way northwards, towards the Somme. Though the French had refused to fight near Paris, it was now increasingly likely that battle would take place. Historians have argued over Edward III's intentions. Did he plan to make a sharp exit, without fighting, or was his whole strategy aimed to draw the French into battle? There used to be a consensus that, sensibly, the last thing that medieval commanders wanted was to fight battles, for that was far too risky. It was far better to concentrate on ravaging an enemy's towns and territories, thereby forcing him to come to terms. However, all of Edward III's propaganda was expressed in terms of engaging the French, and recent argument suggests that the policy of destruction was meant as a way of forcing a possibly reluctant foe to fight in battle. The English army may have advanced northwards from Poissy so as to escape the French; it could also be that Edward III wished to reach the county of Ponthieu, which had been held by the English since the 1270s, but which was now in French hands. To fight on what might be regarded as home ground would give an advantage. No doubt Hatfield was involved in many discussions about the best strategy to adopt, but his views are unknown.

Battle was finally joined in Ponthieu, at Crécy, on 26 August. There, the English drew up their troops on an incline, with the King close to a windmill on the summit. On the opposite side of the valley was a strange feature, a kind of escarpment, about five or six feet in depth. This was quite enough to prevent a cavalry advance; it meant that the French could not march head-on at the English, but had to come into the valley from the side. It also meant that they had no easy way of escape, though that surely did not concern them at the start of the battle. The initial phase saw a force of Genoese crossbowmen advance. However, they did not have all their equipment; in particular, the great *pavises*, movable shields, had not been unpacked from their carts. A crossbowman needed good defence like these, for it took him time to load his weapon. He could only shoot one bolt off in the time a longbowman loosed four arrows. A further problem was that it rained. This made the bowstrings on the crossbows wet, and slack. A longbow, on the other hand, was quick to string; the English archers were able to keep their strings dry until they were needed.

The crossbowmen were driven back, and the French cavalry, eager to advance, rode through and over them. The English archers then caused havoc; horses do not like arrows. They bucked and wheeled, throwing some of their riders. The battle was now fully engaged, and shifted into the mêlée – the indescribable horror of hand-to-hand fighting. There are all sorts of questions about the battle. How were the English organized? The conventional view is that they were in their three battalions, King in the centre, the other two on each side. It is more likely that the Prince of Wales's was in the front, with the other two behind. The archers would have been on the flanks. This means that the brunt of the fighting was borne by the prince's force. Hatfield own position is far from clear, but he was probably in the second battalion, since the King's was to the rear. The chroniclers do not suggest that he was in sole command, but link him with the Earls of Arundel, Suffolk, and Huntingdon, or in one case with Northampton and Suffolk.

The most famous story about the battle, told by the chronicler Jean Froissart, is that of a knight, Thomas of Norwich, coming to the King, to say that the Earl of Warwick, Lord Stafford and Lord Cobham, and the others around the prince were under heavy attack from the French, and needed reinforcements. Edward's response was that he was determined that his son should win his spurs, and did not go to his rescue. A chronicler from Valenciennes provided a different version. The prince was heavily engaged in the fight, and was brought to his knees on two occasions. His standard bearer, Richard FitzSimon, was so alarmed that he put the banner down, and stood on it, so as to prevent it being captured. He swung his sword two-handed, shouting, "Edward and St George! To the king's son!" At this call, Hatfield and his knights came to the rescue. FitzSimon was able to raise his banner again, and the prince was saved. This story does not reveal whether Hatfield actually fought with sword and lance, or used a mace, the traditional weapon for the clergy as it could deliver crushing blows without necessarily drawing blood. This story is wrong about one particular, for a documentary source shows that it was Thomas Daniel, not Richard FitzSimon, who replanted the prince's banner in the course of the fighting, and was duly rewarded for this action. No English writer attributed the rescue of the prince to Thomas Hatfield, but they do not accord the credit to anyone else, which lends some indirect support to the story.

There is, however, an issue about Hatfield and his role at Crécy. On Monday 17 July, according to a formal record, a meeting took place at Newcastle involving Hatfield, the Earl of Angus, Lord Percy, Ralph Neville, Lord Segrave, and others. They agreed to send a messenger to

London to complain to the government that the agreements made with them had been broken, as they had been sent no money. The messenger was also to inform the council in London that a number of lords, as well as the garrison of Berwick, would abandon their posts unless they were paid soon. Segrave said that according to his indenture, if he was not paid within three weeks of reaching Newcastle, he was discharged, and he stated curtly that he would stay no longer. Further, writs summoning parliament, issued on 30 July, assumed that Hatfield was engaged in the defence of the north.

So if Edward III's fleet had sailed for France on 11 July, and the battle of Crécy was fought on 26 August, could Hatfield have attended the Newcastle meeting on 17 July, and still arrived in France in time for the battle? It would have taken at least a week for him to have reached the south of England, and he would therefore have been at least a fortnight behind the King in making his crossing to France. It would have been possible for him to get to Crécy just in time for the battle, in this scenario, but it seems hardly likely.

Hatfield was certainly in France by early September. Pardons were issued to men in the army at his request at this time, one to Hugh son of Adam of Culcheth and another for fifteen men. Later, he also issued a certificate on behalf of Fulk de Bermingham, which testified that de Birmingham had served in the bishop's retinue from the time of the passage to Normandy, at Crécy, and at the siege of Calais. The implication is that Hatfield was present on these occasions, and specifically that he was present at the Normandy landing. However, the St Omer chronicle, a recently discovered and seemingly reliable document, omits Hatfield's presence in the third battalion. On the other hand, the diary of the campaign noted Hatfield's appointment to command of the rearguard, and that is evidence which is hard to dismiss. There is little doubt that Hatfield was on the campaign, and the note of the Newcastle meeting is surely mistaken. It would have been very easy for the clerk who wrote it to have assumed the presence of the Bishop of Durham, even though he was not in fact there.

After the battle of Crécy, Hatfield had a priestly role to play. One of the most tragic and evocative stories of the battle is that of John of Luxembourg, King of Bohemia. He was blind, but his sense of chivalric honour meant that he could do nothing other than fight. With his knights around him, their horses tied together, John charged into the mêlée. After the battle, the dismal sight of the dead king, surrounded by his dead knights, clearly touched hearts. There may also have been regrets over the loss of a king's ransom. There do not seem to have been any great celebrations after the triumph – it seems that even the English were shocked by the scale of the victory, and the sombre mood was reinforced by Hatfield, who conducted a solemn service to mourn the death of the King of Bohemia.

According to the chronicler Jean le Bel and, following him, Jean Froissart, the Queen, accompanied by the Archbishops of York and Canterbury, the Bishops of Durham and Lincoln, and various lay lords such as Percy, Ros, and Mowbray, went to Newcastle soon after the victory at Crécy. On 3 October the Scots assembled their forces outside the town. The English, guided by the Queen, divided their forces into four battalions, with the first led by the Bishop of Durham and Henry Percy. The Queen made an encouraging speech to the men, and went back to safety behind the walls of Newcastle. Battle began with volleys from the archers. Many Scottish nobles were killed. Hatfield captured the Earl of Moray, and the King of Scots, David II, was captured by a Northumbrian squire, John Copeland. So pleased was the Queen with the success of her forces that she kissed her men, one by one. This all took place four days after Michaelmas. Is it possible that Hatfield could have fought nobly at Crécy on 26 August, and then got back to the North of England to fight the Scots on 3 October?

In fact, the battle was not fought outside the walls of Newcastle, but at Neville's Cross, close to Durham. It took place on 17 October, which would have given Hatfield a little more time to get to the battlefield. However, the Queen crossed the Channel on about 10 October for Flanders, and on the day that the battle of Neville's Cross was fought, she was at Ypres, along with her sister Margaret, the Empress. The Earl of Moray was killed in the battle, not captured. Neither the Archbishop of Canterbury nor the Bishop of Lincoln was present. Nor, of course, was Thomas Hatfield. There are a number of letters about the battle, and none mention Hatfield. Indeed, one of these letters was written by the prior of Durham, John Fossour, to Hatfield to tell him what had taken place. So, the account given by le Bel and Froissart is a complete farrago, a demonstration of the inventive powers of medieval chroniclers.

It was, of course, to be expected that Hatfield would have played a part in the defence of the north. That was one of the reasons why he had been appointed to the see; an energetic man, with experience of military organization, was needed. In the circumstances of 1345, when Hatfield became bishop, it must have seemed likely that there would be years of Anglo-Scottish warfare ahead. The battle of Neville's Cross, however, resulting as it did in the capture of David II, put an end to further warfare for some time. Diplomacy replaced fighting. Hatfield was, of course, involved in dealings with the Scots. These did not always go smoothly for him. In 1352 he was appointed to take charge of David II, who had been briefly allowed to return to Scotland. On his way north to receive the Scottish king at Berwick, Hatfield was attacked by an armed band at Morpeth, and detained by them, in what looks like an act of local lawlessness.

By 1355 the Scots were once again threatening invasion. Information had reached the English government that they intended "to perpetrate homicides, destructions, burnings and other evil deeds."[5] In July orders were prepared for the Archbishop of York, who was to recruit men at royal wages, to set out with Hatfield, to attack the Scots should they cross the border. However, the writ was marked as "vacated and nothing was done thereopon."[6] Hatfield, together with Percy and other northerners, made a truce with the Scots, and then went rapidly south to join the King at Sandwich, to take part in an invasion of France. According to a chronicler's account, Hatfield had a force of 100 men-at-arms, 80 armed men (presumably infantry), and 100 archers for this expedition. The Scots, however, broke the truce, overran the English occupation of southern Scotland, and invaded Northumberland. Thomas Gray, constable of the Bishop of Durham's castle at Norham, was captured. News of these events reached the King about all this while he was still at Sandwich, and Ralph Neville was sent back north to deal with the Scots.

The King, however, continued with his plans for an invasion of France, and Hatfield and his force stayed with him. On 2 November the army set out from Calais, and marched south to Hesdin. The French, who had engaged in a scorched-earth policy in order to deprive the English of supplies, marched north from Amiens, and the English retreated back towards Calais. There were the usual challenges to battle, with suggestions of single combat between the two monarchs, but nothing actually took place. The French paid off their army; the English went home. The

5 *Calendar of the Close Rolls, Edward III* – Vol. 10: *1354–1360* (London, 1908), 145.

6 *Calendar of the Close Rolls,* 145.

whole operation had proved singularly pointless. The King then turned his attention to the north. The Scots took Berwick early in November, and Edward retaliated with a savage raid into the Lothians, which became known as the Burnt Candlemas. There is, however, no evidence to show that Hatfield accompanied him on that expedition; it seems likely that the unsuccessful raid to Hesdin was the bishop's final experience of a campaign. He certainly did not go on the great English expedition of 1359; in November a writ explained that the "bishop is now staying upon the safe custody of the march of England against Scotland."[7] By now Hatfield's military career was effectively over. After David of Scotland died in 1371, the situation on the border became more difficult, with the Scots resurgent. There were no major campaigns, however, and given Hatfield's age it is not surprising that he did not play an active part in military action at this time.

One of Hatfield's achievements that needs to be discussed in a military context is his reconstruction of Durham Castle. It was in his time that the great hall was expanded to its present dimensions, and the keep totally reconstructed. The author of the brief fifteenth-century biography of Hatfield, questionably attributed to William Chambre, considered that these changes strengthened Durham's defences, but a keep was an anachronism in military terms. As was the case with much of the castle-building of the fourteenth century, Hatfield's work was more a statement symbolizing power and wealth than a genuine military fortification. Had he been concerned to strengthen the physical defences of the north, it was surely the episcopal castle of Norham that should have received his attention, rather than the palatial building at Durham.

That splendid seal of Hatfield mounted on his charger, heading off to war, was perhaps more an expression of the bishop's hopes than of reality. Hatfield had his part to play in war in the early stages of the Hundred Years War, when he was made a banneret, and campaigned with his retinue alongside the knights of the household. Hatfield's role in the Crécy campaign was a development of this, rather than a consequence of his new position as bishop. No doubt he was appointed to the see of Durham because a man of his experience was likely to be able to deal efficiently with the problem of the Scots; but in the event, the capture of

7 *Calendar of the Close Rolls*, 664.

King David II at Neville's Cross meant that the Scottish threat was far less serious than must have been expected. Thomas Hatfield was a man of military ambition rather than achievement, who as bishop would find other directions in which to fulfil his undoubted talents.

Bibliography

Aberth, John. *Criminal Churchmen in the Age of Edward III: The Case of Bishop Thomas de Lisle*. University Park, PA: Pennsylvania State University Press, 1996.

Ayton, Andrew, and Philip Preston. *The Battle of Crécy, 1346*. With contributions by Françoise Autrand, Michael Prestwich, and Bertrand Schnerb. Woodbridge: Boydell Press, 2005.

Barber, Richard, ed. and trans. *The Life and Campaigns of the Black Prince: From Contemporary Letters, Diaries and Chronicles, including Chandos Herald's Life of the Black Prince*. London: Folio Society, 1979.

Barker, N.A. "'If the King Had Asked for an Ass, He Would Have Received His Wish, This Time': A Study of the Career of Thomas de Hatfield, Bishop of Durham (1345–1381), as a Royal Servant, 1336–1357." MA diss., Durham University, 2003.

Calendar of the Close Rolls. Edward III – Vol. 10: *1354–1360*. London: H.M.S.O, 1908.

Haines, Roy Martin. "Hatfield, Thomas (c. 1310–1381)." In *Oxford Dictionary of National Biography*, ed. H.C.G. Matthew and Brian Harrison, 25: 806–8. 60 vols. Oxford: Oxford University Press, 2004. Online edition: http://www.oxforddnb.com/view/article/12598 (accessed 2 May 2010).

Lyon, Mary, Bryce Lyon, and Henry S. Lucas. *The Wardrobe Book of William de Norwell: 12 July 1338 to 27 May 1340*. In collaboration with Jean De Sturler. Brussels: Palais des Académies, 1983.

Martin, G.H., ed. and trans. *Knighton's Chronicle 1337–1396*. Oxford: Clarendon Press, 1995.

Poulson, George. *The History and Antiquities of the Seigniory of Holderness, in the East-Riding of the County of York, including the Abbies of Meaux and Swine, with the Priories of Nunkeeling and Burstall*. 2 vols. Hull: R. Brown; London: W. Pickering, 1840–1.

Rogers, Clifford J. *War Cruel and Sharp: English Strategy under Edward III, 1327–1360*. Woodbridge: Boydell Press, 2000.

Rollason, David, and Michael Prestwich, eds. *The Battle of Neville's Cross, 1346*. Stamford: Shaun Tyas for the North-East England History Institute, 1998.

Rothwell, Harry, ed. *The Chronicle of Walter of Guisborough*. Camden series 89. London: Royal Historical Society, 1957.

Tout, T.F. *Chapters in the Administrative History of Mediaeval England: The Wardrobe, the Chamber and the Small Seals*. 6 vols. 1920–33; repr. Manchester: Manchester University Press; New York: Barnes & Noble, 1967.

Wardrobe Book, 1334–7. London, British Library, MS Cotton Nero C VIII.

Wardrobe Book, 1340–3. Kew, The National Archives, Public Record Office, E 36/204.

W. MARK ORMROD

Hatfield the Politician

We are all generally aware today of the concept of the "political bishop." In our own times, the label is usually applied to radicals: figures such as Desmond Tutu and Trevor Huddleston in South Africa or, closer to home, David Jenkins of Durham and John Sentamu of York. The political bishop hits the headlines today when he (and soon, perhaps, she) is a dissident, one who challenges the authority and dominant values of the state and champions those oppressed by the laws and culture of secular society. The past, too, generated its fair share of radical episcopal heroes: the obstinate stand taken against Henry II in the twelfth century transformed Thomas Becket, Archbishop of Canterbury, into a national saint; and the burning of Thomas Cranmer in the sixteenth century under Mary I turned another Archbishop of Canterbury into one of the great martyrs of the English Reformation. However, most political bishops during the Middle Ages and the early modern period were, of course, driven by quite opposite instincts. They regarded their responsibility solely in terms of the status quo, of buttressing those triple forces of church, Crown, and parliament on which the English and, later, the British constitutions were founded. Yet we should resist the easy tendency to dismiss establishment-minded bishops of the past as mere sycophants and trimmers. The career of Thomas Hatfield strikingly reveals how a man of highly conservative instincts could still regard himself as the stout champion of the twin causes of church and state.

In Hatfield's own time, the fourteenth century, political bishops tended to manifest themselves in two particular ways. First, there was the powerful phenomenon of the career civil servant who rose through the ranks of secular government and secured high office in the church not so much for his innate suitability as a spiritual leader as for his capabilities as a competent and well-tried administrator. This political take-over of the ecclesiastical hierarchy was itself a symptom of the growing influence of the monarch over senior church appointments and was a cause of some concern among the clergy inside England as well as with the papacy.

The disquiet was articulated mainly in terms of social and academic elitism. Many civil servants who became bishops were born not into fashionable families but into the lower ranks of the gentry and even the upper echelons of the free peasantry; furthermore, they tended not to go to university but to learn the art of government on the job in the great departments of the English state. When these men leapfrogged over those deemed to have the social cachet and academic qualifications suitable for high office in the church, they inevitably created a lot of jealousy. Around the time that Thomas Hatfield became Bishop of Durham, the Pope was beginning to take a more assertive role in such appointments, and many reformers supposed that his involvement would result in a better kind of bishop. In fact, the system known as papal provision operated to the distinct advantage of the Crown. Pope Clement VI's (probably apocryphal) pronouncement on Hatfield's elevation to Durham – "I should have promoted a jackass if the king had nominated one" – reads not as a boast but as an apology to other clerical sensibilities. Nor, I should stress, was Hatfield alone in suffering such jibes: two of his younger contemporaries, John Buckingham and William Wykeham, respectively the Bishops of Lincoln and Winchester, were also initially ridiculed and despised by the English establishment for their lack of higher education.

In contrast to this image of cronyism, the second common manifestation of the political bishop in the fourteenth century emphasized the absolute responsibility of ecclesiastical leaders to promote and defend the liberties of the church. Medieval society was divided by convention into three orders: those who prayed, those who fought, and those who toiled. The clergy, let it be noted, were primary; indeed, since the eleventh century, some clergymen had even argued that their order was superior to the King himself. They therefore had a distinctly high view of their duty to uphold the privileges of their order against the encroachments of the secular arm. The age of Thomas Hatfield marked some of the clergy's last heroic stands on these issues during the Middle Ages, stretching from Robert Winchelsea's confrontation with Edward I in 1296, through John Stratford's dramatic quarrel with Edward III in 1341, to Richard Scrope's execution by Henry IV in 1405. All these men saw themselves very consciously as successors in the tradition of martyrdom set by Thomas Becket. To be a credible bishop in the fourteenth century – and, particularly, to overcome those kinds of social and academic prejudices to which Hatfield and similar others were prone – therefore required that one take one's place at the barricades not in support of some radical social cause but rather as a stout defender of the privileges of the clerical order and the temporal power of the church.

Both of the fourteenth-century manifestations of the political bishop are highly germane to an understanding of the persona and career of Thomas Hatfield. As a former civil servant who owed his elevation entirely to royal favour, Hatfield had no choice but to associate himself strongly with the person and rule of his great patron, King Edward III. Equally, he had the chance to prove his credentials as a faithful servant of the church by identifying strongly with County Durham and its specially privileged status as a palatinate under the temporal jurisdiction of its bishop. Reconciling these two positions was not always easy and caused occasional conflicts not only of jurisdiction but also of personal conscience. Hatfield's ultimate success in negotiating a position between them served to establish him as a figure of genuine stature in the history both of the English state and of the palatinate of Durham.

To start, whatever his place and family of origin and his early training and patronage, Thomas Hatfield first emerges in the records in 1338, when he was appointed receiver of the chamber and keeper of the secret seal to Edward III. These were positions of high influence: we might say that they were comparable to a combination of the roles undertaken today by the private secretaries to the Queen and the prime minister. The promotion was all the more important given the extraordinary conditions of the moment. In 1337 Edward III and Philip VI of France had declared war on each other; no one, of course, knew it at the time, but this was the start of the Hundred Years War. The English Crown shifted much of its focus away from the continuing war with the Scots and towards the impending hostilities on the continent. Between 1338 and 1340 Hatfield was with Edward III in what is now Belgium, helping to build up a great alliance of northern European princes and taking part, as a fighting cleric, in the occasional forays across the border into France. Edward's strategy proved a costly mistake and created bitter tensions between the twin administrations on the continent and at home in England. Hatfield was caught up in the great purge conducted by Edward III upon his dramatic return to England in December 1340 and for a short while seemed to have gone into disgrace. Unlike some of his more abrasive colleagues, however, Hatfield did not arouse the particular ire of the King's vocal critic, Archbishop Stratford. Indeed, rather like Richard Bury, the then Bishop of Durham and another former royal clerk, Hatfield may well have been at work behind the scenes over the winter and spring of 1340–1 trying to generate an amicable solution to the embarrassing public quarrel between the King and archbishop. While Hatfield's efforts remain a matter of speculation, his ability to survive the crisis of 1340–1 surely speaks to a strong sense of judgement and a certain facility in reconciling competing positions.

Edward III's confidence in Thomas Hatfield was certainly sufficient to allow for further swift promotion, and in 1344 Hatfield became keeper of the privy seal. The keeper was at once the mouthpiece of the King's conscience and a prominent member of the council: to emphasize the shift represented by this new title, one might say that Hatfield had moved from being a private secretary to become a kind of home secretary of his day. As things turned out, however, he spent less than a year in this post. In June 1345, at the age of only about thirty-five, Hatfield was appointed to succeed recently deceased Richard Bury as Bishop of Durham. Edward III may initially have thought that Hatfield could continue in both roles. But keepers of the privy seal customarily gave up royal office when they became bishops, and because of its unique jurisdictional status, the bishopric of Durham was not usually considered compatible with high state office. If the King regretted losing a promising civil servant, though, he also knew very well what he was gaining. Richard Bury had demonstrated very effectively that the job of Bishop of Durham was perfectly compatible with maintaining a wider political influence within the King's council and parliament and an influential place in the making of domestic and foreign policy. In reviewing Hatfield's political contribution over the long years of his tenure at Durham, then, it is useful to think about his activities at three levels: the local, the provincial, and the national. We might express these levels in terms of three corresponding locations: the city and county of Durham, the North of England, and Westminster.

County Durham, the liberty of St Cuthbert, was a unique political entity in the Middle Ages: a palatinate, in which virtually all royal authority was delegated to the bishop, who then ruled the county in his own right. When Hatfield became bishop, there was only one other palatinate in England, the county of Chester, held by the eldest son of the monarch. In 1351 a third was created in Lancashire, under Edward III's cousin Henry of Grosmont, Duke of Lancaster. The establishment of this palatinate was meant chiefly as a mark of special honour to a senior nobleman who had performed conspicuous service in the Scottish and

French wars. It was also a reminder of the original strategic considerations that had led to the creation of the older palatinates of Chester and Durham, namely, the need to establish powerful political leaders in areas close to the borders with Wales and Scotland who would assist the Crown in delivering stable government and effective defence.

Given the circumstances of 1345, then, there is every reason to believe that Thomas Hatfield was appointed to Durham chiefly to ensure that the resources of the bishopric and county would be mobilized in the service of Edward III's war with the Scots. This war, begun in 1332–3 with the battles of Dupplin Moor and Halidon Hill, had led the English King to place a puppet monarch on the throne of Scotland in the person of Edward Balliol. By the mid-1340s, however, Balliol had been driven out of the northern kingdom and replaced by the young David Bruce, son of Robert the Bruce and, by the estimation of most people north of the border, the true King of Scots. The resurgence of the Bruce regime made it increasingly difficult to hold the sequence of truces in place since the late 1330s, and by 1345 the North of England was once again subject to quite serious cross-border incursions. It was imperative, then, that the new Bishop of Durham be the kind of man who could take an appropriate lead in the government and defence of the North of England.

The major issue for Hatfield, and for the inhabitants of County Durham as well, was the extent of the support that the county ought to provide to English royal enterprises against the Scots. Durham was immune both from providing compulsory military service outside the palatinate and from paying taxes to the Crown. It is quite clear that the gentry of Durham liked the status quo and expected the bishop to defend their little tax haven in the north. Hatfield's predecessor had taken a rather different view and had complied quite readily with the Westminster administration in imposing his own charges on County Durham. In his eagerness to prove his credentials and uphold the privileges of the palatinate, Hatfield ended up fighting a fierce campaign against the wishes of the English parliament and the royal exchequer, in defence of what he regarded as the absolute fiscal independence of Durham. (One of the interesting anomalies of Hatfield's position, it should be noted, is that the clergy of the county and bishopric, who paid separate taxes, did not enjoy the immunity sustained by their counterparts among the laity.) While the rest of England suffered a sustained period of direct taxation through the later 1340s and 1350s, then, Durham remained remarkably untouched at least by the pressures of lay taxation. It may be suspected that in holding his ground so notably on this matter, Hatfield was further motivated by the appalling levels of human suffering he witnessed among his subjects in the palatinate as a result of the onset of the Black Death in 1348–9 and its recurrence in subsequent decades.

This issue of taxation came to a head in 1371 when the Crown once more challenged the privileged status of the palatinates and, under pressure from parliament, attempted to levy a special new tax, known as the parish subsidy, in Durham. Hatfield's hostile reaction could no doubt have been predicted. Nor was he alone: to some degree, his protests chimed with those of other bishops in this period, such as the outspoken William Courtenay of Hereford, who were coming to argue that the country simply could not sustain the continuing commitment to Edward III's foreign adventures. In 1374 the Crown finally had to concede that its attempted intrusions into the palatinates were not to be taken as a precedent and thereafter withdrew its efforts to tax the liberty of Durham. Hatfield could be considered lucky; had things gone another way in 1345 or in 1371, his episcopate could easily have become known as the beginning of the end of the privileges of County Durham. As it was, his later biographer William Chambre had good justification for counting among Hatfield's many virtues a proper tenacity in promoting the rights of the land of St Cuthbert.

Enough has already been said to indicate that Thomas Hatfield played a conspicuous role not just in the government of County Durham but also in the more general political leadership of the North of England. There is, of course, a central irony to Hatfield's record as defender of the north: the bishop's participation in the major continental expedition mounted by Edward III in 1346 meant that he was not able to join the great encounter between the English and the Scots that took place that same year at Neville's Cross. Rather, it fell to Hatfield's superior, William Zouche, Archbishop of York, to provide the clerical presence among the leading lords of the realm who gathered outside Durham to see the Scots off and celebrate John Copeland's brilliant accomplishment of capturing David Bruce. It might indeed be suggested that much of Hatfield's striking self-image as a martial figure – the mounted warrior on the seal, the rebuilding of the castle and other city defences, and so on – was a retrospective attempt to have the public imagination associate him with the great missed opportunity of his northern career in 1346, the battle of Neville's Cross. That he went at least some way towards achieving this convenient rewriting of history is demonstrated by the fact that some later chroniclers simply assumed that he must indeed have been present at Neville's Cross.

Rather than dwelling on his missed opportunity of 1346, however, it might be rather fairer to stress that Hatfield's major claim to fame in the northern wars was not as a soldier but as a peacemaker. The negotiations with the Scots that followed the capture of their king at Neville's Cross ground on for an astonishing eleven years, during most of which time David Bruce lived the high life of an honoured house guest of the English court. Finally, in October 1357 terms were agreed upon in an Anglo-Scottish conference at Berwick. Hatfield was there and, with other northern English lords, formally confirmed the treaty of Berwick on behalf of Edward III. David Bruce was to be released from captivity, and so long as his government continued to pay the regular instalments of the ransom established for his delivery, a state of truce would remain. Not surprisingly, Hatfield became heavily involved in the preservation of this truce as one of the Wardens of the Marches, the group of northern ecclesiastics and lords appointed to organize the patrolling of the border and to arbitrate the frequent squabbles that broke out between inhabitants living on either side of that fragile line.

The other important dimension to Hatfield's provincial role in the north came as a result of his relationship with the metropolitan jurisdiction of the see of York. Then, as now, the English church was divided into two provinces under the presidencies of the Archbishops of Canterbury and York. When Hatfield became Bishop of Durham, there was still a good deal of rivalry, and sometimes open hostility, between the two archbishops over whether their status was equal or whether Canterbury could claim seniority over York. Although there was a notable easing of this position in the 1350s as a result of an accommodation between two former keepers of the privy seal lately turned archbishops, John Thoresby of York and Simon Islip of Canterbury, the northern province continued to enjoy a good deal of autonomy. In particular, it kept its own clerical parliament, or convocation, which met once or twice a year, usually at York Minster. Convocation dealt with matters of doctrine and discipline. It was also the body that gave formal assent to royal taxes imposed on the clergy of the north and the place where the clergy drew up formal lists of complaints and requests which they sent on to the King in the hope of gaining statutory concessions confirming their rights. The records of the northern convocation are patchy, but there is every reason to believe that here, as in the governing of County Durham, Bishop Hatfield aimed vigorously to uphold the rights of the church against the encroachments of the state. Given his earlier experience in government and his obvious sensitivity on matters of taxation, indeed, it is tempting to see him as something of a "fixer" in the political negotiations between the northern province and the royal government, especially during the period up to 1356, when John Thoresby was generally constrained by his obligations as lord chancellor to uphold the interests of the Crown. Of his facilitating role, furthermore, one might suspect that Hatfield once more applied his mediatory abilities from 1340–1 when he successfully negotiated a balance between the unrealism of some of his episcopal colleagues and the pragmatism that he identified as better serving the purposes of their order.

The main interest concerning Thomas Hatfield's status and activity in the province of York, however, involves his markedly tense and at times openly hostile relationship with three successive archbishops, William Zouche, John Thoresby, and Alexander Neville. If Hatfield thought that their common civil service background would create effective working relations with Zouche and Thoresby, he was quickly thwarted. In 1349 two members of Hatfield's household, William Legat and John Grey, were accused of creating a great disturbance in York Minster. And in 1358 Thoresby accused Hatfield of organizing an armed attack on one of the archbishop's servants. Finally, in 1360 the root cause of the trouble became apparent when one of the earlier agitators, John Grey, now Hatfield's chancellor, made a remarkable statement during the convocation of York. The Bishop of Durham, he argued, ought to be completely exempt from the jurisdiction of the Archbishop of York. In law and precedent this was, to say the least, a highly dubious claim. But Hatfield was all the more confident because he knew that he had the Crown on his side. In 1375 when the new archbishop, Alexander Neville, announced his bold intention to make a visitation of the diocese of Durham, Hatfield had the aged Edward III issue a stinging denunciation of the action as being in direct contravention of the autonomous traditions of the liberty, bishopric, and county of Durham. The acrimony between Durham and York might seem to us no more than a waste of time as well as an excuse for gratuitous bad behaviour. In terms of what it did for the status and reputation of the diocese and palatinate of Durham, however, the humiliation of Archbishop Neville in 1376 did, indeed, represent one of Thomas Hatfield's finest hours.

To address Hatfield's third area of public activity, his involvement in national politics, we move from the northern environment to London, and more specifically to the Palace of Westminster, which by the 1340s had become the established headquarters for the principal offices of state and for meetings of councils and parliaments. Hatfield's regular treks to the capital are attested in the official register of his deeds as bishop, which records the number of regular pastoral and jurisdictional functions within the diocese that were fulfilled by substitutes appointed in his absence. The practical challenges of such frequent travel are certainly not to be taken lightly. If he went by horse via the Great North Road, it could easily take a week to get from Durham to London; if he went by boat around the east coast and up the Thames, as he did on at least one occasion, the journey might be either significantly shorter or much longer, depending on winds and tides. It is hardly surprising, then, that Hatfield wanted somewhere comfortable and private to stay when he eventually reached the capital. Significantly, he built a new townhouse for the Bishops of Durham, first known as Old Ford and later as Durham House, in a fashionable location off the Strand.

Hatfield's regular appearance in London facilitated his involvement in international affairs. The skills he acquired in Anglo-Scottish affairs were readily transferrable to the Anglo-French arena, and Hatfield had a role in some of the great set pieces of fourteenth-century diplomacy. In 1360 he was among the distinguished group of English lords and bishops who travelled to Calais to confirm what Edward III hoped would be a lasting settlement to the French war. After that treaty finally collapsed in 1369, Hatfield was once more deployed in cross-Channel negotiations. In the summer of 1370, for example, he travelled to war-torn Normandy to stand surety with the Earls of Suffolk and Warwick for a visit to the English court by that most slippery of Edward III's fellow rulers, Charles the Bad, King of Navarre. As the older generation of military commanders and ambassadors died off in the 1360s and early 1370s, Edward III surely came to rely quite significantly on Hatfield as one of very few men whose personal knowledge of his great enterprise in France stretched right back to its original inception in 1337, when he first declared war.

Hatfield's stature as a national politician is best demonstrated in parliament. By the mid-fourteenth century, parliament had already emerged as a bicameral institution of Lords and Commons. It was still an occasion rather than an institution and usually convened only once a year for a period of two or three weeks. The bishops sat alongside the earls and barons in the Lords in their common capacity as tenants-in-chief of the Crown; the Commons were made up of elected representatives of the shire counties and an increasing number of cities and towns. Unless there was some striking piece of business to be done, many backwoodsmen among the Lords often stayed away, and at times there were probably only around twenty or thirty peers present in active session. In Hatfield's case, however, there is good evidence not just of regular attendance but also of real activity and influence. The King often held private conferences with the Lords, away from the larger body of the Commons, and it was during such confidential negotiations that much high policy, especially relating to the course of the Scottish and French wars, was conducted. That Hatfield was regarded as what we would now call a working peer is best shown by his regular appointment to the committees of Lords set up in each parliament to help the Crown clear the mass of private business, submitted in the form of petitions from the King's subjects across England and the wider dominions of the Crown. In the period from the 1350s to the 1370s, virtually no other bishop sat so regularly or for so long on such special commissions as Hatfield. Indeed, his commitment continued right up to the end of his life; the last parliament that Hatfield attended was held at the unusual venue of Northampton in November 1380. Here, above all, we see the signs of the bishop's remarkable ability to endure the long haul of political life.

Hatfield's involvement in business of state also allowed him to maintain at least some form of social presence at court. During much of Hatfield's tenure as Bishop of Durham, the court of Edward III observed a kind of official season based around the great sequence of spring-tide religious festivals and having at its heart the annual gathering of the Order of the Garter, Edward III's own chivalric foundation, at Windsor Castle on 23 April. When events in the life cycle of the royal family were to be celebrated or when foreign potentates needed to be impressed, Edward III could also roll out full-scale court extravaganzas, including religious services, feasts, balls, masques, and tournaments. Clerical sensibilities could certainly be offended by the scale and manner of such celebrations: Hatfield may have shared others' outrage when the King's eldest son, Edward, the Black Prince, chose the Seven Deadly Sins as the theme of the London tournament held to celebrate his marriage to Joan of Kent. On the whole, however, Hatfield's early service in the royal household and his own inclination towards the virtue of magnificence surely made him an enthusiastic participant in court life. In 1355 he stood as principal godfather – and thus gave his name – to the King's last child, Thomas of Woodstock. A decade later he was one of those who received a personal invitation to attend the nuptials of the King's eldest daughter, Princess Isabella, at Windsor Castle. This last event was probably the very pinnacle of courtly extravagance in the period; Edward III's expenditure on wedding gifts alone came to the equivalent of the annual income of a wealthy earl. These glimpses of the bishop's involvement in the social calendar of the royal family provide the most powerful indicator we have that the early association between Edward III and Thomas Hatfield had blossomed in their middle age into a real and lasting bond of personal friendship.

Curiously enough, it is this close and abiding connection with the court that was also to prove the greatest challenge of Hatfield's long and varied career. The last decade of the bishop's life coincided with the emergence of serious factionalism in the circle of the ageing Edward III. The general decline in the King's health and strength coincided with a serious reversal in English fortunes in the war with France, and in the face of huge demands for taxation, the political community began to fixate on what it saw as corruption in high places. One of the major foci of complaint was the King's mistress, Alice Perrers. Apart from the scandal of her public liaison with the King – she appeared at a famous tournament in London in 1376 dressed as the "Lady of the Sun" – Perrers was also a highly ambitious woman whose operations on the credit and property markets often brought her into conflict with the male elite. Not the least of those caught up as unwilling parties and victims in her wily business deals was Bishop Hatfield.

By the early 1370s Thomas Hatfield had amassed a considerable personal fortune which, as a loyal servant of the Crown, he agreed to invest back into the King's military enterprises in the form of war loans. Unfortunately for him, this spate of lending coincided with a crisis of public finance which left many of Edward III's creditors unsatisfied. Like others, Hatfield sought Alice Perrers's assistance in securing repayment and was prepared to hand over several County Durham manors to gain her support. All his effort was to no avail. After Edward's death in 1377 and Perrers's exposure and disgrace, Hatfield would complain bitterly to the new regime of the boy King, Richard II, that Perrers's sharp practices had left him out of pocket to the considerable sum of 1,000 marks (£667), equivalent to the annual income of a wealthy baron. Hatfield was far too much of a loyalist to withdraw and sulk, though; like other peers and prelates in 1377, he felt very strongly that the elite had to pull together to overcome the scandals of Edward III's last years and support the minority government of King Richard. It is hard to escape the feeling, however, that Hatfield found the going at in court distinctly tough with his advancing old age.

Herein, then, lay the dichotomy of Thomas Hatfield's political career. By instinct and experience Hatfield was a royalist, scrupulously loyal in his personal service to Edward III and his public allegiance to the Crown. It was this commitment, reinforced by a degree of genuine affection between the bishop and the King, that also provided the surest guarantee of the rights and privileges of Hatfield's palatinate of Durham. Like many members of the elite, Hatfield believed that the problems of the 1370s could be overcome if only the English elite could reunite around the values of Edward III's hey-day and engage once more in confident and successful prosecution of the war with France. Unlike some of his fellow prelates and lords, moreover, Hatfield was prepared to put real personal investment and effort into such an enterprise.

Ultimately, however, it must be admitted that he was simply conspiring in a collective delusion that refused to acknowledge either the disastrous reversal of England's military fortunes or the unsustainable burden that foreign war now placed on a fragile and shrinking economy. Flailing out at Alice Perrers was, therefore, only a distraction from the much bigger systemic problems that faced the English Crown after 1377. It was at Hatfield's last parliament, in November 1380, that the polity took the final and most disastrous action in a series of badly misjudged policy decisions and imposed the notorious third English poll tax. While the laity of County Durham remained safe behind their wall of tax immunity, the rest of England was about to be faced not only with a tax strike but also with that greatest public indictment of Crown policy in the whole of the Middle Ages, the Peasants' Revolt of June 1381. It was in the interim between these fateful events that Thomas Hatfield died, full of years, at his London townhouse on 8 May 1381.

It is perhaps rather difficult for modern audiences to feel much empathy for Bishop Hatfield. One can certainly marvel at the vigour and persistence with which he pursued a career in public life over more than forty years. One can also admire the considerable skill with which he maintained that delicate balancing act between his loyalty to the Crown and his leadership of the liberty of St Cuthbert. However, the quarrels with the Archbishops of York and with Alice Perrers also reveal the less attractive sides of his character: the tendency to always pull rank and yet to inhabit the moral high ground, a certain obsessive quality, and more than a whiff of vindictiveness. Even the Durham monk William Chambre had to admit that Hatfield was inclined to self-importance. Those are surely also the characteristics captured in that most remarkable statement of Hatfield's world view, his tomb on the south side of the choir in the Durham Cathedral. Yet it would clearly be a mistake to judge Hatfield simply by the standards of our own time. Hatfield demonstrated both the clarity of vision and the sense of judgement which, at least until the 1370s, allowed him a highly successful and influential place in the public life of the realm. Were we able to ask him what he felt his finest achievement as a political bishop was, there can scarcely be any doubt that he would respond in terms of his uncompromising allegiance, over a remarkable thirty-six-year tenure, to the bishopric and palatinate of Durham.

Bibliographic Note

In addition to Thomas Hatfield's register, housed in the Durham University Library, and the registers of the relevant Archbishops of York, held at the Borthwick Institute for Archives, University of York, much of the archival evidence for Bury's involvement in the convocation of York is collected together in *Records of Convocation*, ed. Gerald Lewis Bray, 20 vols. (Woodbridge: Boydell Press, 2005–6). The main primary sources for Hatfield's career in secular politics are the various published and unpublished records of royal government preserved at The National Archives (TNA) in Kew. The evidence for his civil service career is thoroughly analysed by T.F. Tout, *Chapters in the Administrative History of Mediaeval England: The Wardrobe, the Chamber and the Small Seals*, Publications of the University of Manchester, Historical series, 6 vols. (Manchester: The University Press; London and New York: Longmans, Green & Co., 1920–33). The omission of Hatfield from the witness lists to royal charters after 1349 means that his influence on central politics has tended to be underrated: see Chris Given-Wilson, "Royal Charter Witness Lists, 1327–1399," *Medieval Prosopography* 12 (1991): 35–93. The evidence of his attendance at councils and court events and in diplomatic missions can be gleaned from unpublished expenses accounts (TNA, E 101) and issue rolls (TNA,

E 403) and from occasional chronicle notices such as those in *The Anonimalle Chronicle, 1333–1381, from a Ms. Written at St. Mary's Abbey, York, and now in the Possession of Lieut.-Col. Sir William Ingilby, Bart.*, ed. V.H. Galbraith, Publications of the University of Manchester, Historical series 45 (Manchester: The University Press; London: Longmans, Green & Co., 1927). His conspicuous service in parliament can be tracked in *The Parliament Rolls of Medieval England, 1275–1504*, gen. ed. Chris Given-Wilson, 16 vols. (Woodbridge: Boydell Press; London: National Archives, 2005), and has been the subject of analysis by Gwilym Dodd, *Justice and Grace: Private Petitioning and the English Parliament in the Late Middle Ages* (Oxford and New York: Oxford University Press, 2007), 91–108. For Hatfield's protection of the special fiscal status of Durham, see W.M. Ormrod, "An Experiment in Taxation: The English Parish Subsidy of 1371," *Speculum* 63 (1988): 58–82. And for his conflicts with Archbishop Neville and Alice Perrers, see Christian D. Liddy, "The Politics of Privilege: Thomas Hatfield and the Palatinate of Durham, 1345–81," in *Fourteenth Century England, IV*, ed. J.S. Hamilton (Woodbridge: Boydell Press, 2006), 61–79; and W. Mark Ormrod, "The Trials of Alice Perrers," *Speculum* 83 (2008): 366–96.

1 Detail of crest on the tomb of Bishop Thomas Hatfield, Durham Cathedral

2 Detail of crest on the tomb of Bishop Thomas Hatfield, Durham Cathedral

3 Detail of crest on the tomb of Bishop Thomas Hatfield, Durham Cathedral

4 Detail of crests on the tomb of Bishop Thomas Hatfield, Durham Cathedral

5 View of tomb of Thomas Hatfield and Bishop's throne, Durham Cathedral

CHRISTIAN D. LIDDY

Hatfield the Bishop

It is almost impossible to speak of Thomas Hatfield simply as a churchman and bishop. For in the late Middle Ages, Durham was no ordinary episcopate: it was also a palatinate. The Bishop of Durham was not just any other bishop: he was also, as King Edward III described Bishop Thomas Hatfield in 1376, "earl palatine," a rather exotic title of continental provenance, which was first used to honour the Bishops of Durham in the late thirteenth century.

What kinds of powers did a bishop like Hatfield exercise? Spiritual powers, naturally. The diocese of Durham stretched between the rivers Tees and Tweed. Thomas Hatfield's ecclesiastical register is a thorough record of his activities as diocesan and of the operation of his diocesan administration.[1] It contains information about the appointment of the clergy to benefices and the ordination of candidates to priesthood. All of these duties were routine and expected of a diocesan bureaucracy, whatever the identity and wherever the location of the episcopal see. Hatfield, like bishops in other parts of England, also enjoyed secular power by virtue of the estates, lands, and properties that belonged to the see of Durham. Much is known about Thomas Hatfield's role as landlord from an estate survey compiled towards the end of his episcopate.[2] But Hatfield further inherited powers that other bishops did not possess. He was the ruler of the palatinate of Durham. This was a geographical territory that stretched between the rivers Tyne and Tees, as well as south of the Tees into Yorkshire and north of the Tyne into Northumberland. Within the palatinate, the bishop enjoyed powers normally reserved to the English Crown in other parts of the kingdom. This was a region where the

1 Register of Bishop Hatfield, Durham Cathedral Muniments, Durham University Library.

2 *Bishop Hatfield's Survey: A Record of the Possessions of the See of Durham, Made by Order of Thomas de Hatfield, Bishop of Durham*, ed. William Greenwell (Durham, London, and Edinburgh, 1857).

King's writ did not run. The Crown's commands had to be communicated via the bishop, and even then they were not always obeyed.

Justice in the palatinate was enforced in the name of the bishop, not the King, through a system of courts housed on the Durham peninsula between the castle and the cathedral. Here, too, just like the King in Westminster, the bishop had an exchequer and a chancery (a writing office), which produced a plethora of documentation now preserved in The National Archives in Kew. How the Bishops of Durham ended up in this peculiarly powerful position, we still do not know. Hatfield knew that Durham was different from most other places in England because of its status as a palatinate. It was Hatfield who introduced a new great seal, which was attached to documents emanating from his chancery. On one side was the bishop seated in majesty on the episcopal throne, dispensing justice and the power of mercy, and on the reverse was the bishop clad in armour, sitting on a horse, with a sword by his side. Two things strike me as especially interesting about these images. First, Hatfield's seal was self-consciously modelled on the King's great seal. (Other Bishops of Durham, incidentally, followed Hatfield's example, so he can be regarded as an innovator in this respect.) Just as the royal seal communicated the idea of the King as upholder of justice and defender of the realm, so Hatfield's seal conveyed the message that he – not the King – was both peacemaker and defender of the palatinate. Second, what distinguished Hatfield from the King is the fact that he appears on horseback with a mitre on top of his helmet – the mitre, of course, being a symbol of his spiritual authority. In this respect, the equestrian image of Hatfield recalled the much-quoted statement about Bishop Antony Bek, Hatfield's predecessor in the early fourteenth century, that "there are two kings in England, namely the lord king wearing a crown in sign of his regality, and the lord bishop of Durham wearing a mitre in place of a crown in sign of his regality in the diocese of Durham." If Thomas Hatfield could do things that neither his colleagues on the episcopal bench in England nor lay magnates – earls and barons – could, is it any wonder that it was said of Hatfield (and here I quote from a contemporary description that is now the Hatfield College motto) that he "always strove to be first or among the first" in any aristocratic gathering? Who could blame Hatfield for thinking that he was a rather important and powerful person?

Indeed, Thomas Hatfield, from the moment he became bishop, would have been very aware of the distinctive nature of his new position.

When Hatfield headed north in the summer of 1345 to assume his office as Bishop of Durham, he would have participated in a rather extraordinary inaugural ceremony involving the head of the Conyers of Sockburn, a knightly family whose members had held the manor of Sockburn, located in the most southerly tip of the diocese, since the early twelfth century. Here, on the bank of the Tees, after the bishop crossed the river for the first time, Hatfield would have been handed a curved sword, known as a falchion, which he would then be expected to return immediately to the person who had presented it. The Conyers falchion, which is on display in the cathedral treasury, dates from the mid-thirteenth century. The sword was both a symbol of title – lacking written documentation, the Conyers maintained it in their possession as proof of their ownership of the manor of Sockburn – and a peculiar form of land tenure, since the Conyers held the estate of Sockburn in return for showing their ancient sword to each new bishop on his appointment. Another context for the presentation of the Conyers falchion to Hatfield lies in the bishop's ceremonial interaction with his new subjects. The sword was delivered to Hatfield as part of his *adventus*, his first formal entry into his jurisdiction upon his assumption of episcopal power. Later evidence suggests that the occasion of the bishop's crossing of the river Tees was usually accompanied by trumpets and acclamation from the Durham clergy, gentry, and others.

More than that, we need to recognize the giving of the Conyers falchion to Hatfield as one element of a sequence of rituals that inaugurated his rule. Upon his arrival at Auckland Castle, the palatinate's main episcopal residence since its reconstruction in the late thirteenth century, Hatfield would have been met by another reception party. This one involved a minor gentry family known as the Pollards, who occupied a house in the market square of Bishop Auckland, where they kept a ceremonial falchion of their own. Evidence from the fourteenth century – precisely Hatfield's era – reveals that the Pollard falchion was given to the bishop "on his first arrival (*in primo adventu suo*) at Auckland after his consecration." The swords belonging to the Conyers and Pollards were delivered to and returned by the bishop in an exchange that acknowledged the bishop's special temporal powers within the palatinate as overlord from whom all the inhabitants held their land. These rituals of inauguration were the secular counterpart to the ecclesiastical process of consecration and enthronement in Durham Cathedral. It may be going too far to infer a deeper symbolism in Hatfield's acceptance of "two swords," but might this sequence have also alluded to the medieval church's doctrine of the divided powers of church and state and to their custody now by one person?[3] Viewed together, the rituals surrounding these two swords would have constituted an impressive reception for Hatfield. Bishop Auckland was no Rome or London. I cannot find evidence of any triumphal arches in the streets of Bishop Auckland. If a comparison between Hatfield's ceremonial entry into Durham and that of Roman emperors and English kings into their capital city for the first time is slightly invidious, we can nevertheless speak of a kind of provincial *adventus* for Hatfield. Durham's cultural traditions, displayed upon his arrival in the palatinate, would surely have made an impact on Hatfield. It is too easy to criticize the high opinion that the bishop had of himself; it was justified by his reception.

What follows in the rest of this chapter is an attempt to locate Hatfield primarily within his local (or regional) milieu. My argument is simple: within the context of the historical, political, and cultural development of the palatinate, it is extremely difficult, on the one hand, to speak of Hatfield purely as a bishop, that is, to disaggregate his ecclesiastical status from the territorial, political, and administrative powers he exercised in north-east England; and, on the other hand, to separate his activities as secular ruler of the palatinate from his role as bishop.

A good example of the symbiotic roles of bishop and earl palatine is Hatfield's use of spiritual sanctions to fortify his secular authority. Just like the King, who from the eleventh century had particular hunting rights in an area known as the royal forest, the Bishop of Durham owned areas of forest that were administered by officials on his behalf. Besides two massive deer parks at Stanhope and Wolsingham, the Bishops of Durham had in their possession the forest of Weardale, an area covering the entire Wear Valley from Stanhope in the west to Bishop Auckland in the east. In 1378 Hatfield's chief forester came to see him at Auckland Castle to complain that several "sons of iniquity" (in the words of the document), whose names he did not know, had broken down the fences and gates of the Wolsingham deer park. Thomas Hatfield responded to the complaint with a sentence of excommunication against the unknown offenders and ordered the vicar of the parish church of Wolsingham to publish the sentence. In the same year, one of Hatfield's sub-

3 I owe this suggestion to my colleague, Dr Len Scales.

foresters petitioned the bishop and informed him that, once again, certain unknown men of iniquity had entered Weardale forest without his consent or that of the bishop and furtively removed certain birds of prey, destroying the birds' nests in the process. Hatfield wasted no time in ordering his archdeacons to issue in all the churches of the bishop's diocese a spiritual censure, that those responsible for the theft should restore the birds to the bishop's forester or else face excommunication. When individuals who had committed crimes might not otherwise be identified through the normal legal channels, Hatfield was clearly prepared to call upon the power available to him as head of the northern church.

There is further evidence of the blurring of the boundaries between the bishop's secular and ecclesiastical roles in the identity of those Hatfield chose to administer and run the palatinate. Like any other magnate, whether lay or ecclesiastical, Hatfield had a retinue made up of people who served him in various capacities and who looked to him for lordship and patronage. Hatfield's household, whose members were in almost constant contact with the bishop, provided the backbone to his retinue. This was also true of the retinues of great lay magnates, such as dukes and earls. Bishop Hatfield's household was very different from those of great secular lords due to its distinctively ecclesiastical character. It contained a staff of clerks and chaplains whose attendance upon Hatfield was predicated primarily upon the need to help him discharge his spiritual duties as diocesan. What is really striking in the case of Thomas Hatfield is that these very men were also his most trusted advisers in temporal matters. The people who actually held the main secular offices in the palatinate were clerical servants within his household.

The most important post within Hatfield's palatine regime was that of steward. He was the bishop's deputy and main adviser in the governance of the palatinate. Just below him in the office hierarchy was the position of temporal chancellor, whose occupant was in charge of the writing office from which all documents concerning the palatinate were issued. The office of steward of Durham during Hatfield's episcopate was filled by an uninterrupted sequence of clerks and chaplains, who were also deans of Bishop Auckland, archdeacons of Durham, and vicars general when the bishop was absent from his diocese. Similarly, the post of temporal chancellor, which was held simultaneously with the offices of constable of Durham Castle and receiver of the exchequer, was monopolized by members of the clerical estate. For almost the entirety of his episcopate, Hatfield's palatine chancellors were all clerks from his household. Since Hatfield himself was a cleric, are his choices for these positions surprising?

Hatfield's appointments tell us something of the elusive character of the man. The pattern of appointments after Hatfield's tenure threatened to undermine Durham's episcopal autonomy. This trend, as the elevation of Robert Neville to the see of Durham in 1438 suggests, involved the increasing influence of the major lay aristocratic family in the palatinate, the Nevilles of Raby and Brancepeth, on local political life. After Hatfield, there was a single lineage system in Durham in which the resources of the palatinate (grants of office and land) were placed firmly at the disposal of one family for its own benefit. It became virtually impossible to separate the Bishop of Durham's retinue from the affinity of the Neville family.

Bishop Hatfield's episcopate was different. The relationship between Hatfield and John Neville, Lord of Raby, the most powerful lay magnate in the palatinate and also the King's steward, was cordial, but there were also tensions generated by the fact that Hatfield had his own affinity. These tensions are revealed in a curious episode, the full details of which remain obscure. The case revolved around the theft of a substantial sum of money from the palatine exchequer at Durham towards the end of the 1360s. Since the exchequer was located at this time within the bishop's castle, where building work was underway, the main suspects were the masons who were under the supervision of the bishop's chief mason, John Lewyn. In 1371 the main suspect, a mason by the name of Richard Goldesburgh, secured a royal pardon from Edward III upon the request of John Neville. A year later, Hatfield ignored the King's pardon and Neville's support for the suspect. He ordered his own sheriff to arrest and imprison Goldesburgh and his master, John Lewyn. Lewyn found himself accused of harbouring the mason pardoned the year before by the King, and he was indicted, imprisoned, and tried before the bishop's justices at Sedgefield in 1372. Hatfield was most definitely his own man.

That Hatfield appointed churchmen to the key posts in his palatine administration and that clerical members of his household held such influence within the bishop's secular service partly reflected Hatfield's desire for loyalty. These men were the bishop's clerks, and their ties to Hatfield were personal and binding. They enjoyed an intimacy with the bishop as members of his household. These clerks were also of a professional class whose skills and expertise were valued by Hatfield because they were expected to lead to the more efficient administration of the palatinate. In some ways, this conclusion is hardly surprising: the Oxford Dictionary of National Biography's entry for Thomas Hatfield describes him succinctly as "administrator and bishop of Durham," which is an interesting ordering of priorities. Hatfield was a good administrator.

But what does this mean? One way to answer this question is to ask, why did efficiency and administration matter to Hatfield? It could be said that they helped to maximize the bishop's revenue from his estates and from the myriad sources of income which belonged to the bishop both as diocesan and as ruler of the palatinate. It could also be argued that such revenue was essential to enable Hatfield to live the aristocratic life to which he always aspired. In short, Hatfield was a landlord just like any other member of the aristocracy in this period. Some of the revenue undoubtedly went towards the extensive building projects for which Hatfield was remembered locally. Hatfield financed the construction of the bishop's hall and constable's hall in Durham Castle and of a new tower to strengthen the city walls of Durham. Such munificence involved a strong element of social display, and Hatfield, it could be claimed, was acting exactly like the heads of major families in the palatinate, including the Lumleys of Lumley Castle, the Hyltons of Hylton Castle, and the Nevilles of Raby and Brancepeth, all of whom rebuilt their residences in the second half of the fourteenth century.

Yet there is another aspect to Hatfield's role as administrator which deserves attention and which highlights the difference between great lay lords and clerical lords. Their obligations were different. The point about all these lands – and the authority the bishop exercised over them – is that they belonged to the bishop primarily as custodian of the church of Durham. The precise genesis of the palatinate is shrouded in mystery. There is no single point from which the palatinate can be said to have come into existence. The palatinate developed organically and gradually, building upon the pre-Conquest piecemeal accumulation of property by the church of Durham in the name of St Cuthbert. The land between the rivers Tyne and Tees constituted, and was frequently called, the patrimony of St Cuthbert, within which the saint was believed to exercise special powers to protect it from outside interference. In 1344, the year before Hatfield became bishop, King Edward III sent a couple of royal commissioners to Hartlepool to conduct an inquisition into the death of the local lord. The inhabitants of Hartlepool refused to cooperate with the King's officials on the grounds that they lived in the liberty of St Cuthbert, where a writ of the King did not apply, and they threatened the royal officials with the sentence of excommunication which St Cuthbert would undoubtedly impose, presumably through the person of the bishop, if they tried to continue their investigation.

The Bishops of Durham had a specific responsibility to maintain and administer their landed estates because these territorial possessions were dedicated and belonged symbolically to St Cuthbert. Just as bishops were the successors to the Apostles and the Pope was the successor to St Peter, the Bishops of Durham were expected to imagine themselves as the lineal descendants and earthly representatives of St Cuthbert and as the temporary custodians of the endowments of his church. Lands, and the rights which accompanied landholding, could not be permitted to be lost; any loss was often expressed in terms of damage to the "holy body of St Cuthbert and of his church of Durham." Conversely, since land was the basis of their palatine powers, the Bishops of Durham were also supposed to be determined defenders of palatine privilege and autonomy. This was land which in origin had been granted to St Cuthbert, most of it posthumously, and which continued, in a sense, to be regarded as Cuthbert's possession into the later Middle Ages. The logic of Hatfield's decision to draw on his spiritual powers and clerical household to buttress and augment his governance of Durham should now be clear. Palatine privileges and traditions were bound up in the ancient possessions of the church of Durham and in the person of St Cuthbert, the founding figure of that church. Hatfield, like all Bishops of Durham, had a duty to safeguard the interests of St Cuthbert.

It should be said that some later medieval Bishops of Durham took their responsibilities as the successors of Cuthbert more seriously than others. One way to demonstrate this is to examine the bishop's itinerary. Where did Hatfield spend most of his time? Can we detect a pattern to his movements? Hatfield's itinerary can be reconstructed from his bishop's register. The register is unpublished and is not an easy read. It is the product of his spiritual chancellors and consists largely of matters relating to Hatfield's role as diocesan, including grants of indulgences and licences for private chaplains. The vast majority of these acts, recorded in the name of the bishop, provide details of the place where they were issued. There are gaps in Hatfield's register, notably for the period from 1345 to 1350, but evidence elsewhere indicates that he was in regular attendance at the royal court during these years. Thereafter, Hatfield disappears entirely from the records of the King's court. Hatfield was occupied with business in the north-east, principally the area bounded between the rivers Tyne and Tees. He seems to have spent well over three-quarters of his episcopate in the region. He could never be accused of being a "non-resident" cleric, a charge that was made against two of his immediate successors, John Fordham, who replaced Hatfield in 1381, and Walter Skirlaw, who supplanted Fordham in 1388. Fordham was made treasurer of the royal household in 1386, whilst Skirlaw was valued by Richard II and Henry IV primarily as a diplomat and therefore had to make many trips abroad, especially to France. When the fifteenth-century prior of Durham, John Wessington, asked the then Bishop of Durham, Thomas Langley, to enforce the terms of an ancient agreement regulating relations between the bishop and the chapter of Durham Cathedral Priory, he complained that it had been very difficult to speak to Langley's predecessors, Fordham and Skirlaw, since they had "resided almost continuously in London."

In contrast, apart from his regular attendance at parliament – as bishop, he received a summons to the House of Lords – Hatfield otherwise lived in his diocese. His longest absence from Durham occurred in 1376, the year of the Good Parliament, which saw for the first time the use of the parliamentary process of impeachment against the King's ministers and the refusal by the House of Commons to grant taxation to the King. The Good Parliament lasted longer than any previous parliamentary assembly (ten weeks), and Hatfield was away from his diocese for about five months. The best example of Hatfield's typical itinerary comes from 1378. He was at Bishop Auckland almost continuously from February of that year through to October, when he was in Gloucester to attend a parliament. Of all his episcopal residences – including Howden in the East Riding of Yorkshire, Crayke in North Yorkshire, and castles at Stockton, Bishop Middleham, and Darlington – Auckland Castle was his favourite. Of course, Hatfield's routine residence within his diocese did not necessarily make him a "good" bishop, a conscientious diocesan. We do not know whether he was more preoccupied with spiritual than secular affairs. Perhaps this is a question *mal posée*. What do these categories mean, particularly in a Durham context?

There is, however, a more pressing issue. How should historians evaluate the performance of a bishop? By which criteria should he be judged? These are important questions. Hatfield does not seem to have had a reputation for great personal piety, in contrast to some of his contemporaries on the episcopal bench such as Ralph Shrewsbury, Bishop of Bath and Wells, whose episcopate lasted for thirty-four years (only two fewer than that of Hatfield). The Oxford Dictionary of National Biography's entry for Ralph Shrewsbury highlights his status as a saintly bishop, whose pastoral activities made him, in the eyes of modern historians, an "exemplary medieval bishop." Shrewsbury's episcopal register contains entries, dating to the immediate aftermath of the Black Death in the mid-fourteenth century, which describe the bishop issuing orders to the clergy of his diocese to organize prayers and processions to secure God's forgiveness for the sins of the laity and making ad hoc arrangements for laymen to confess their sins to other laymen, since so many priests had died of the plague. So far as I can tell, there is no evidence of such pastoral care in Hatfield's register, although this conclusion is qualified by the gap in the register for the critical years of 1345 to 1350. Unlike his predecessor, Richard Bury, Hatfield is not known for his love of books and learning. Whereas Bury collected books, established a large private library, and gathered around him a dazzling array of Oxford theologians, Hatfield was neither a book collector nor a patron of scholarship and was not noted for having any particular interest in theology.

In evaluating Hatfield's merits, I have not considered the visitations he conducted within his diocese to ensure that the standards of the clergy remained high, his relations with the cathedral priory of Durham, or what might be regarded as the purely spiritual side of his duty as bishop. Hatfield's register does contain dispensations for absence awarded by the bishop to members of his clergy, which authorized them to leave the diocese to study at Oxford. From this evidence, other historians could begin to construct an argument about the extent to which Hatfield was interested in the subject of clerical education, a possibility that is perhaps given even more credence by his legacy of £3,000 towards the support of a college at Oxford for eight monks and eight secular clerks.

The reason for these omissions is because Hatfield's true achievements as bishop lay elsewhere: in his role as defender of the ancient liberties and privileges of Durham. He always acted to prevent what he described as the "disinheritance" of St Cuthbert. Hatfield's episcopate was characterized by his vigorous defence and preservation of Durham's traditional autonomy. He protected the palatinate from the burden of royal taxation, buying off the Crown's attempt to raise money from Durham in 1345 and lending a total of £3,000 to the Crown in the early 1370s to prevent his subjects from having to pay tax to the King. The strategy was a success. The hated poll taxes of the late 1370s, which provoked the Peasants' Revolt in 1381, were never imposed in Durham. Hatfield's actions were those of a man who took seriously his obligations to maintain the privileges of the palatinate because they were so closely associated with the rights of the church of Durham and with the figure of St Cuthbert in particular. The enforcement of rights and duties and the determination to ensure that lands and privileges committed to their care were never usurped or lost – were not these part and parcel of being a Bishop of Durham? Hatfield also displayed concern for the pastoral welfare of his subjects. If he was keen to enforce his rights, he was aware of the need to act in the interests of those he ruled. In 1357 Hatfield organized a wide-ranging judicial commission to investigate allegations of malpractices perpetrated by the bishop's officers since the beginning of his episcopate in 1345. He responded to his subjects' complaints by removing his chief minister. Bishop Hatfield never faced the kind of constitutional crisis within the palatinate which his successor, Thomas Langley, experienced in the 1420s and 1430s, when the bishop's subjects revolted against the heavy hand of palatine lordship.

Is this chapter open to the charge of trying to whitewash Hatfield? Hatfield certainly had a high opinion of himself. His magnificently ornate two-storey funerary monument in the choir of Durham Cathedral, consisting of the effigy of the bishop on an altar tomb situated below his episcopal throne, speaks of someone with obvious pretensions. Durham, however, was different. The peculiar conglomeration of spiritual, territorial, and regal powers exercised by Thomas Hatfield was not matched by any other English bishop of his day. Hatfield, to his credit, knew that Durham was different. He should be remembered as he was locally during his lifetime: a bishop who "defended, to the best of his ability, the rights of the liberty of the bishopric against outsiders."

Bibliography

Greenwell, William, ed. *Bishop Hatfield's Survey: A Record of the Possessions of the See of Durham, Made by Order of Thomas de Hatfield, Bishop of Durham*. The Publications of the Surtees Society 32. Durham: George Andrews; London: Whittaker & Co., and T. & W. Boone; Edinburgh: William Blackwood and Sons, 1857.

Liddy, Christian D. *The Bishopric of Durham in the Late Middle Ages: Lordship, Community and the Cult of St Cuthbert*. Woodbridge: Boydell Press, 2008.

—. "Land, Legend and Gentility in the Palatinate of Durham: The Pollards of Pollard Hall." In *North-East England in the Later Middle Ages*, ed. Christian D. Liddy and Richard H. Britnell, 75–95. Woodbridge: Boydell Press, 2005.

—. "The Politics of Privilege: Thomas Hatfield and the Palatinate of Durham, 1345–81." In *Fourteenth Century England, IV*, ed. J.S. Hamilton, 61–79. Woodbridge: Boydell Press, 2006.

Register of Bishop Hatfield. Durham, Durham University Library, Durham Cathedral Muniments.

RICHARD H. BRITNELL

Bishop Hatfield's Legacy

Thomas Hatfield's legacy, like many legacies, is mostly a matter of bits and pieces. To assess that legacy and to put it in its context, I begin with a few words about the man in question, who rose from a modest Yorkshire family through royal service to hold one of the most valuable bishoprics in England.

From his position as the King's secretary, Thomas Hatfield was elected Bishop of Durham on 8 May 1345, when he was probably in his mid-thirties, and remained bishop until his death on 8 May 1381, soon after he had attained his full three-score and ten. He was sometimes away from Durham on the King's service. Even as bishop he had many secular responsibilities, both as lord of the palatinate and as one of the King's principal councillors in northern England, and was obliged to appoint clerical deputies to carry out his more routine episcopal duties. He was, nevertheless, ultimately responsible for the management of the diocese in troubled times. In 1349, four years into his term as bishop, the Black Death swept the diocese, reducing its population by about a half and creating difficulties for Hatfield both as a bishop and as a secular lord. During the same period, Edward III was waging the series of wars with France known retrospectively as the Hundred Years War, which began in 1337. In the course of his thirty-six years as bishop, warfare abroad and social change at home created numerous problems to be coped with. Hatfield died a matter of weeks before the great explosion of resentment we call the Peasants' Revolt. That was a southern affair and not an event in which his tenants became involved, but there are numerous signs of stresses and strains of other sorts amongst the villagers on the bishop's estates throughout the third quarter of the fourteenth century. In the church, too, there were major upheavals to negotiate, most notably the Great Schism that began in 1378 when two popes were elected simultaneously, the Italian Urban VI and the French Clement VII. An administrator of talent like Hatfield was highly valued as a bishop at the best of times, but even more so in times of exceptional uncertainty.

Hatfield's roles as soldier, politician, and bishop have been explored in previous chapters, and I have no intention of discussing further those aspects of his career. My topic invites, rather, a discussion of their fallout. Let us first begin by examining what an earlier writer thought of his lasting legacy. This comes from an account of Hatfield's career written as part of a compilation known as the *Continuation of the History of Durham*. Though attributed in Raine's edition to a fourteenth-century author, William Chambre, *Continuation* was probably written in the later sixteenth century. Its quality is not wonderful, but it will do well enough as a peg on which to hang the topics I wish to discuss.

Continuation's author singles out for first mention, as indeed we might today, the construction in Durham Cathedral, beyond the choir stalls, that combines Hatfield's tomb and Durham's episcopal throne. This is the most public memorial to Hatfield's self-esteem. "He built," we are told, "a remarkable construction on the south side of the cathedral choir beside the monks' stalls. In the middle he made the bishop's stall and appropriately furnished it. It was surrounded with images finely carved at great expense by workmen who were handsomely paid. Beneath this was a place for his tomb, where he lies buried with dignity." The throne was restored in about 1700 by Bishop Crewe and repainted in 1772 by Bishop Egerton, so none of the original decoration has survived. It is often said to be the highest bishop's throne in Christendom, though others say more cautiously that it was claimed as the highest at the time it was built. Who was it who had travelled through Europe to collect the evidence for such claims, either in the fourteenth century or later?

By the nineteenth century, the tomb below the throne had lost most of its original paintings and its inscription. Robert Billings indicated that the tomb had been whitewashed and then scraped, so that almost all traces of paint and gilt had been obliterated; the drawings of the tomb that he first published in 1841, and later included in his *Architectural Illustrations* of 1843, show hardly any sign of decoration. The once-fine alabaster effigy had been mutilated, and the tomb had been boarded up on the choir side. Most of the present painting and gilding dates from 1933 to 1936. It was probably then, too, that the small inverted angels on the segmental arch over the choir side of the tomb were renewed. They are absent in Billings's earlier engraving of the tomb from the choir side, which shows a long and ornate pew hard up against the tomb. The prior destruction of the inverted angels on the tracery cusps, according to Billings, had been a deliberate measure "to gain head-room." His picture of the tomb on the aisle side shows the original angels still in place.

The design of the tomb allowed it to be used as a chantry where masses could be said for Hatfield's soul. The *Rites of Durham* tells us that a little altar adjoined the tomb "which he [Hatfield] prepared for a monk to say mass for his soul after his death, the altar being environed with an iron gate." Billings identified the site of this altar as a niche on the left-hand side of the tomb, on the aisle side, "where one of the Norman shafts was cut away to make room for it." This is shown in his etching.

Pevsner had mixed feelings about Hatfield's monument, pronouncing, on the one hand, "as a composition it is unique," but, on the other, "as a work of art it lacks imagination." His problem with it seems to be that it is stylistically rather old-fashioned, especially compared with the nearby Neville Screen, which was completed shortly before Hatfield's death and probably designed by Henry Yevele, England's best architect of the time. Since Hatfield's tomb was given the monks' approval long before his death, its design presumably corresponded to Hatfield's taste. So maybe we should conclude that Thomas Hatfield was grandly original in his ambitions but somewhat conservative in his appreciation of the arts. Just to show that beauty is in the eye of the beholder, however, I can quote to you Billings, who in 1843 described its ornamentation as "exquisitely chiselled" and opined that "where there is so much beautiful form, artificial colouring is quite of secondary importance." I can quote, too, Canon Greenwell, who in 1857 thought the "splendid" throne and tomb were "monuments of [Hatfield's] taste and munificence."

The author of the *Continuation* then discusses other works of significance at the time. Like many major prelates of the Middle Ages, Hatfield was a great builder and repairer of buildings. He reconstructed parts of Durham Castle, notably by reshaping the bishop's hall and the constable's hall. The former is, of course, the present hall of University College. He extended the hall southwards so that it was even bigger than it is today; it was later reduced in size by Bishop Fox, who converted the extension into various offices. The most impressive surviving feature of Hatfield's development is the hall's timber roof. Other constructions of Hatfield's, though they lasted well, no longer stand. For example, he strengthened a tower that was part of the castle, possibly the shell keep on the castle mound. The author of the *Continuation* indicates that this was done to enhance the fortifications of the city. However, the tower was destroyed in 1840.

Hatfield's tomb, his other constructions, and his great seal were marked at the time with his coat of arms, described as "azure, a chevron or between three lions rampant argent." The coat of arms, too, has had interesting subsequent fortunes. It was informally adopted by Hatfield Hall when it was founded in 1846 and has remained at the core of the Hatfield College arms through successive modifications. The College added the bracing motto *Vel primus vel cum primis*, taken from the description of Hatfield in the *Continuation*: "His sense of grandeur was such that in meetings of the noble and powerful he always strove to be the first or amongst the first." Amongst Hatfield's legacies in the medieval period is the decisive influence of his coat of arms on that of the bishopric of Durham, which was first known from a mid-fifteenth-century episcopal seal of Robert Neville's. Though the seal was created many years after Hatfield's death, its episcopal arms are a simple modification of Hatfield's, with lions around a central cross rather than a central chevron. Another of Hatfield's legacies is the present armorial of Durham County Council, which is essentially a secularized version of Neville's episcopal coat of arms. The latest version displays a small Yorkshire white rose in the middle of the cross, added in 1974 when the county acquired Startforth Rural District from the North Riding.

Hatfield also built a chapel and chambers at his palace in London, probably about 1345. This was the bishop's palace, which stretched from the Strand to the Thames, was long retained by the bishops as their London base, and was later known as Durham House or Durham Inn. There is still a street in the area called Durham House Street. The bishop's palace was a sufficiently noble building to accommodate King Henry IV as a guest. The grounds towards the river were extensive. Eventually the palace was surrendered by Bishop Tunstall to Henry VIII, who gave it to Princess Elizabeth. The house was rebuilt for its royal owners, and there is no surviving picture of its earlier form. Durham House survived as a recognized location until 1769–70, when it was demolished to make room for the Adelphi Buildings.

In the fourteenth century, Durham Priory distinguished itself in the world of learning by maintaining a small hospice in Oxford to which monks were sent to study. Canterbury Cathedral Priory was the only other English monastery with a similar commitment. Durham had had its own accommodation for monks probably since the 1280s and had produced some notable scholars, John of Beverley and Uthred of Boldon.

Hatfield's episcopate was a turning point in the history of this establishment. At the instigation of Robert Walworth, the prior, Hatfield re-endowed Durham College on Broad Street, Oxford, with a rich legacy of £3,000, yielding an annual income of £133 6s. 8d., to provide for the accommodation of eight monks. In addition, the endowment would house eight secular undergraduates – four from Durham, two from Northallerton, and two from Howden – to study at the College for seven years. In this way, Hatfield provided for the needs of both the monks and the secular clergy. He died before the final arrangements had been made, and building work did not begin until sixteen years after his death. However, the ordinances he drew up for the College in 1381 were used as the basis for the College statutes. The refounding of Durham College perhaps deserves to be remembered as Hatfield's most important legacy, since besides serving to educate Durham monks and Durham undergraduates for over a century, the buildings were eventually incorporated into Trinity College, Oxford. The eastern range of the Durham Quadrangle there contains the library, which dates from 1420 and can therefore be regarded as an indirect and posthumous consequence of Hatfield's bounty.

The author of the *Continuation* was interested in Hatfield's more ephemeral legacy to the monks of Durham, which he lists in loving detail. Hatfield, he states, died a rich man, and some of those riches came the priory's way: horses and other livestock, ecclesiastical vestments and altar cloths, a gilded silver crucifix, sacred vessels and candlesticks, and furnishings for their hall. He gave them an honoured relic, a thorn from Christ's crown of thorns, which had been given to him by the King. As an interesting demonstration of his commitment to episcopal magnificence, he also left £200 to buy jewels because the existing episcopal finery seemed to him inadequate.

Most of these legacies are matters of historical report, leaving little trace for us today. In fact, the contemporary second-hand account I have been citing does not include the surviving objects from Hatfield's episcopate that are most valued by modern historians. I refer to the surviving records from his time as bishop. Every fourteenth-century English bishop kept administrative records, and there is nothing particularly remarkable about Hatfield's, which were mundane, utilitarian, and, at the time of his death, had no monetary value. After six hundred years, though, the availability of such records cannot be taken for granted; as historical artefacts, they are no longer mundane or utilitarian, and they have a rather high monetary value, which is why they are carefully preserved in libraries and record offices.

The surviving administrative records of Thomas Hatfield's are few but notable. In general, the survival of the bishopric of Durham's records is disappointing for the period before the 1400s. It is not known whether this was simply because they were badly looked after, whether they met with some accident, or whether they were deliberately destroyed. Apart from the important late twelfth-century survey of the bishop's estates known as *Boldon Book* and a number of episcopal charters that survive in other collections, there is virtually nothing left of what must have been at least a century of archive material from before 1300. Even for the fourteenth century the survival rate is poor: some chancery rolls, some inquisitions into the estates of deceased tenants, and all in rather bad condition. This is a pity, because it means that bishopric records are not available for the study of such major fourteenth-century events as the Scottish invasions after the battle of Bannockburn in 1314, the famine of 1315–8, and the Black Death that reached Durham in 1349. However, the poor survival rate inevitably enhances the value of those records of this period that have survived, some of the most important of which are from Hatfield's time.

The Bishop of Durham was head of several separate administrations, all of which required copious record-keeping. The first concerns his episcopal duties. His agents in Durham maintained an active correspondence with fellow clergymen on a variety of issues. They had to record episcopal visitations of the priory and other churches and ordinations of new clergy (a particularly active area of concern in the aftermath of the Black Death). They were also required to supervise the apparatus of the ecclesiastical courts in Durham; the bishop's consistory court had authority over testamentary bequests, matrimonial disputes, sexual offences, heresy, and slander. The principal legacy of all this activity from Hatfield's time is a bishop's register preserved in Durham University Library. The record survived badly, and there are gaps between 1345 and 1350 and again between 1355 and 1359. Nevertheless, it deserves more attention than it has so far received. Apart from a fragment of Bishop Bury's register, it is the earliest Durham bishop's register extant.

A second administrative system, unique to the Bishop of Durham, involved his responsibility as palatine lord of Durham. Because of his exceptional authority, he was responsible for administering institutions in a manner parallel to the royal administration at Westminster. The bishop's chief concern here was with jurisdiction. He was obliged to enforce the common law of England, except insofar as it was incompatible with his rights. He sent out writs and kept track of lawsuits that passed through his court on Palace Green. The bishop's chancery rolls are the most important surviving legacy of this jurisdiction; the extant series begins in 1333 under Hatfield's predecessor, Bishop Bury, and runs almost continuously until the sixteenth century. Hatfield's episcopacy is well documented in two rolls. Their contents are extremely varied. They contain details of private lawsuits brought to the bishop's chancery, which corresponded in this respect to the King's chancery at Westminster, and some private deeds relating to contracts and recognizances that individuals paid to have registered in the bishop's court. They also contain an assortment of matters of administrative relevance. In particular, the chancery rolls record appointments to public office in the palatinate, commissions to the bishop's justices and other offices, and instructions to the Durham sheriffs. We learn, for example, that very early in his episcopacy, Hatfield appointed a commission to raise £400 to buy off the King, who had proposed during the vacancy following Bishop Bury's death to send justices into Durham to remove pleas from of the bishop's control. Most other records relating to palatinate jurisdiction, such as assize rolls, have been lost. However, there is a single sheriff's account that is the earliest surviving record from Hatfield's time.

A third administrative responsibility was required of the bishop as one of England's major landlords. The bishop and the priory, between them, owned a large part of modern County Durham. The patrimony of St Cuthbert had long been divided into two separate landed estates, one to maintain the priory and one to maintain the bishop, an arrangement that Hatfield confirmed in 1354. Both estates were nevertheless large and required regular attention to collecting rents, finding tenants, corresponding with local agents, and resolving tenurial problems. Unlike a modern landlord, the bishop had a measure of police jurisdiction over his customary tenants, which he exercised through a system of halmote courts held at various points across the estate three times a year. Most of the archival material relating to this activity is lost. There are no general receivers' accounts until 1384, after Hatfield's death, and no collectors' accounts before 1398.

On the other hand, there are two major estate records from Hatfield's time that deserve particular attention, especially since his name is permanently associated with one of them. We have the earliest surviving records of the halmote courts held on the bishop's manors during Hatfield's time. These are very remarkable. Usually records of courts like this were kept on parchment rolls, sewn together, and were generically known as manorial court rolls. They are one of our principal sources for studying medieval rural society, since they contain not only details of litigation between country dwellers concerning acts of violence and debt but also matters relating to local policing, the management of agricultural operations, and relations between lords and tenants. Because they were compiled on separate membranes of parchment sewn together and because it is in the nature of stitching to come undone in the course of six centuries, series of fourteenth-century court rolls are often very incomplete. Once the membranes have come adrift, they become spoiled or get mislaid or thrown away as unidentified litter. It then becomes difficult, at best, to construct a continuous picture of court business from what remains.

By the time the Durham bishopric halmote court records began in 1348, however, details of halmote court proceedings were being systematically copied from the original court rolls onto parchment sheets that were then bound into registers. These survived intact better than rolls, and as a result the court records are complete for many years in succession. Even more helpful is that the bishops kept records for all their halmotes in the same registers, so that we have a complete series for the whole of the bishopric estate. The first surviving register runs with no losses from 1348 to 1362. There is then a gap of twenty-six years, so we do not have a record for the latter part of Hatfield's episcopate. It is true, too, that some of the more ephemeral material that was in the original court rolls was edited out by the clerk who copied the court proceedings into the register, and the original rolls are lost. Nevertheless, matters relating to relationships between the bishop and his tenants have been retained in these records for a critical period in the history of the estate following the Black Death, when relations between landlords and tenants were particularly fraught. Consequently, we have from Hatfield's time one of the best documented instances of how a major landlord coped with a massive loss of tenants and a severe decline in land values.

Another eponymous legacy of Bishop Hatfield does not have the widespread acclaim of Hatfield College and is less well known to art historians than Hatfield's tomb, but the text known as *Hatfield's Survey* is one of the most important records of society in the medieval north-east.

Compiled in Hatfield's last years, between 1377 and 1380, with later insertions made after his death, it provides a complete survey of the bishop's estate. The only comparable record of the bishopric estate is *Boldon Book*, compiled nearly two hundred years earlier. So *Hatfield's Survey*, invaluable as evidence of the estate as it was around the late 1370s, also allows us to explore how things had changed over the thirteenth and fourteenth centuries. It includes details of all the bishop's manors, which were numerous; lists all the tenants and the rents or services that they owed; and records other episcopal assets like water mills and forges. The *Survey* survives precariously in a single copy that was previously used by the bishop's auditor and is now preserved in The National Archives in Kew. It was edited for the Surtees Society by William Greenwell in 1857 but now needs re-editing to conform with modern standards and improved information.

As these comments suggest, much of Hatfield's legacy has been lost through time, and even the artefacts that survived are in need of more attention if they are to be as useful as they could be. These things will happen in time. In the meantime, it is a pleasure that Hatfield College has taken this opportunity to keep Hatfield's memory fresh, and I hope that this book, which has come out of the series of lectures held at the College in 2010, will encourage the College to take more to heart the distinguished man after whom it is named.

Bibliography

Billings, Robert William. *Architectural Illustrations and Description of the Cathedral Church of Durham*. London: T. and W. Boone, 1843.

Greenwell, William, ed. *Bishop Hatfield's Survey: A Record of the Possessions of the See of Durham, Made by Order of Thomas de Hatfield, Bishop of Durham*. The Publications of the Surtees Society 32. Durham: George Andrews; London: Whittaker & Co., and T. & W. Boone; Edinburgh: William Blackwood and Sons, 1857.

Haines, Roy Martin. "Hatfield, Thomas (c. 1310–1381)." In *Oxford Dictionary of National Biography*, ed. H.C.G. Matthew and Brian Harrison, 25: 806–8. 60 vols. Oxford: Oxford University Press, 2004.

Larson, P.L. *Conflict and Compromise in the Late Medieval Countryside: Lords and Peasants in Durham, 1349–1400*. London: Routledge, 2006.

Pevsner, Nikolaus. *County Durham*. 2nd ed. revised by Elizabeth

Williamson. 1983; repr. New Haven and London: Yale University Press, 2002.

Piper, A.J. "Chambre, William (fl. 1365?)." In *Oxford Dictionary of National Biography*, ed. H.C.G. Matthew and Brian Harrison, 10: 1010. 60 vols. Oxford: Oxford University Press, 2004.

Raine, James, ed. *Historiae Dunelmensis scriptores tres, Gaufridus de Coldingham, Robertus de Graystanes, et Willielmus de Chambre*. The Publications of the Surtees Society 9. London: J.B. Nicols and Son, and William Pickering; Edinburgh: Laing and Forbes, 1839.

Appendix One

N.T. WRIGHT

Wisdom and Hope: A Sermon by the Bishop of Durham

(Proverbs 8.1–11; Matthew 6.25–34)

A sermon at evensong on the eve of Hatfield Day, 14 June 2010, in the Cathedral of Christ, Blessed Mary the Virgin and St Cuthbert, Durham, by the Bishop of Durham, Dr N.T. Wright.

I am delighted to have this opportunity to celebrate the eve of Hatfield Day with you.

I have long felt grateful for the fine example set by Bishop Hatfield, my predecessor by nearly seven hundred years. Last time but one that I was in Rome, I took care to have a photograph of myself taken in front of the great papal throne in St Peter's, precisely so that I could gloat over the fact that it is a few inches smaller than Hatfield's throne here in Durham, which is so high that on the rare occasions when the bishop ascends it, he always takes an extra handkerchief in case of nosebleeds.

Among the many things that Hatfield is famous for is, of course, his mustering of the great army for the battle of Neville's Cross in 1346 – the army which assembled in the Bishop's Park at Auckland, where now I'm afraid all I can muster is an Anglican golf team to take on our Roman Catholic neighbours. (So far we usually lose.) Among my many regrets at the abolition of the status of Prince-Bishop in the 1830s is that ability to raise a private army, which would have come in handy on several occasions, and, indeed, the equal ability to mint one's own coinage to pay them.

How times have changed; though since the battle of Neville's Cross was fought against the Scots and since I am shortly on my way to live and work north of the Tweed, I feel slightly differently about it all now, as indeed about the wing in my house called the Scotland Wing, in which Hatfield and other medieval bishops used to keep their Scottish prisoners.* History is always informative but often, in my experience, surprisingly ironic.

However, we are here today to celebrate and thank God not simply for Bishop Hatfield himself, worthy though he was and is of that, but for the College that for a hundred and sixty-four years has borne his name, here on the Bailey.

In these days of educational institutions springing up like plants in the night, and sometimes disappearing like that as well, it is a great thing to belong at whatever level to a foundation whose continuity can be traced back to the time before Einstein had discovered relativity, before Wagner had composed the *Ring*, and before Darwin had published the *Origin*. And, of course, before anyone had thought about atom bombs, holocausts, Internet pornography, or any of the other "delights" that our wonderfully enlightened modern world has dreamed up for us. Life was often quite hard in first half of the nineteenth century, but they were spared some of the real horrors of our day.

The traditions of Bishop Hatfield himself were continued by the founders of the College. Hatfield was a generous man, who used the then very considerable resources of the bishopric – now sadly all administered by bureaucrats in an office in London – for serious work of charity right across this region, remembering that until the late nineteenth century the diocese of Durham ran all the way up to Berwick-upon-Tweed. The foundation of the College made it clear, in what was then an innovative and ground-breaking move, that every effort should be made to accommodate and educate even such students as were not themselves able fully to afford such a thing.

Today we face fresh challenges in higher education, with governments once again casting greedy eyes on the universities as soft targets for stringent financial measures. We should be prepared to stand up and say that the hopes of people like the Reverend David Melville, your founder, should not be forgotten and that this country and the world as a whole would have been massively the poorer had it not been for the generations of students over the last 160 years who have gone out from Hatfield College, having received a splendid education which their own means would not have permitted them to afford. We forget these tradi-

* [Editor's note: The Bishop of Durham left the see of Durham on 31 August 2010 to take up an appointment to a research chair at the University of St Andrews, Scotland.]

tions of philanthropy at our peril. Again, smartly dressed people in London may not always remember that in places like Durham (surrounded by the real poverty of former pit villages, former steel and railway towns, and former shipbuilding industries, all now the victims of social and political manoeuvrings elsewhere), we have an obvious calling, social as well as theological, to be a beacon of hope for all around, not only for those few who can afford to purchase as a privilege what ought still to be bequeathed as a birthright.

I say this not simply because it is an obvious reflection both on Hatfield himself and on the motives of the founders of the College that proudly bears his name. I say it because today's Bible readings have a strong note of hope, and hope is what so many in our society notoriously lack. In the Sermon on the Mount, whose central section formed our second lesson, Jesus commands his followers not to worry. They are not to go about with long faces, saying, "What shall we eat?" or "What shall we drink?" or "What shall we wear?" I have to say that two of those, at least, strike me as exactly the sort of question you might hear around a college at a certain time of a certain evening, as the men lay in stocks for the bar and the women worry about whether someone else has bought the identical dress from Next. As for eating – well, the common table was a feature of Hatfield College from the beginning, and having enjoyed its hospitality on more than one occasion, I don't expect it is any less splendid now than then.

The point of the Sermon on the Mount is a hope born of faith: a hope for the future that grows out of a strong and emphatic awareness of God not as a faceless bureaucrat but as a loving Father. It is not just an awareness; it is something to work at and strive for. "Seek first God's kingdom and his righteousness," says Jesus, "and all these things will be yours as well." God's kingdom means, briefly and bluntly, the fact that God is running the show, even though it may not look like it, and that we are called to be people through whom that healing, challenging divine sovereignty is lived out in our relationships, in our academic work, in our plans for the future, in our common life. College life, in fact, is an excellent, if challenging, way of getting to know how the world works and of discovering the difference that a robust and cheerful faith in God as Father actually makes.

There are few places to hide in a college; most people know you and you know most people, and vices and virtues are on display day and night. A college such as yours actually sends a signal of hope into a world that badly needs it. Because for many people, these days, "home" is not such a cosy or secure place as it used to be, and for some, indeed, the community you find in a college may be the first such place, and perhaps also the last such place, where you will live in close daily contact with dozens or hundreds of others who will, broadly speaking, accept you, enjoy your company, challenge you when you say outrageous things, ask you your opinion, invite you to sing in a choir, cajole you into rowing in a boat, and generally value you for all sorts of things, some of which you knew about and others of which you did not. I was talking recently with a senior naval officer who said that they now assumed that with many of their intake of junior sailors, this was going to be the first time these young people, many from deprived backgrounds, had been part of any properly functioning community at all, and they learnt quickly what was expected of them.

It may not be quite so stark as that in a college, but part of the virtue of college life – and I mean "virtue" in the full technical sense, of the habits of heart and mind which form the person you become – is that you learn to take care of one another, to be there for one another, to hold on to one another's worries and troubles. That may not take us all the way to fulfilling Jesus's bracing command not to worry at all, but it may be a signpost which points towards a world in which we are looked after, [but] at the same time [are] being challenged not to be lazy but to seek God's kingdom first and above all things. If people from Hatfield College are supposed, according to your College motto, to be either first or among the first, it's worth remembering that in Jesus's teaching, God's kingdom is always first. When you get that sorted, you discover that faith and hope are basically team sports: you have to play your part, but you play it alongside all the others who are learning it together. Do not, then, take membership of a college for granted. It is a rare privilege, and I hope you are making the most of it. Much is expected of those to whom much is given.

The other Bible reading this evening matches the Sermon on the Mount stride for stride. The ancient Hebrew book of Proverbs contains hundreds of individual proverbs, sharp little nuggets of good advice that will see you through many a tight spot. But rising up above these hundreds of little words of wisdom, much as Durham Cathedral rises up above the hundreds of little buildings clustering around the Bailey and in the wider town, we see a central figure, Wisdom-in-person: a great lady, standing beside the cross-roads and beckoning to the simple to come to her and learn instruction and knowledge. Of course, Wisdom is more than the accumulation of facts or the ability to manipulate laboratory equipment; more again than picking up another couple of languages or theorems or learning off a few clever theories about what Shakespeare really meant. Wisdom is about something that transcends, though it may well include, all that. It is about seeing the larger picture, and seeing it so clearly that it becomes second nature, so that you are not blown off course by the latest foolishness, of which we have an abundant supply today not least through cheap-and-twittering technology, and so that you are not fooled by clever but specious arguments. Wisdom is something that you acquire as you live within a community and discover more about how human life works than you had expected to. It is about discerning where the line between responsibility and frivolity must be drawn. It is about discerning which patterns of behaviour build up a community and which patterns destroy it. Many people never have the chance to learn the wisdom that comes through community life. You have that opportunity for a brief moment, and again I hope you make the most of it.

At the centre of the Wisdom tradition is the strange truth which we only discern gradually: that Wisdom is not a quality, but a person. Wisdom in Proverbs is God's agent in creation, the one through whom all things were made. Discovering Wisdom means discovering not only the Father who made you and loves you, but God's second self, as it were, the one who comes alongside, often incognito, and whispers to you that this is the way to become genuinely human and that the other way leads over a cliff. And as the passage goes on, beyond where we stopped this afternoon, we discover that this Wisdom is what you need if you are to run a country, or a business, or a court of law, or (we might add) a hospital, or a ship, or a rugby team. Wisdom is the personal presence of the God who made the world and knows, from the inside, how it works best. In a world where different messages are being shouted at us all the time, pulling and pushing us this way and that, it is an excellent thing to pause, as we do today, and celebrate the fact that the God who made the world longs to give us that Wisdom, to give us his own presence and guidance, to transform our follies and failings so that, bit by bit, we are able to become more fully what we were made to be: humans, reflecting God's image to the world around.

We who call ourselves Christians claim to know the personal name of this Wisdom, this "second self" of God the creator. It was one of the most striking and astonishing things about the early Christians that they came quickly to believe that Jesus himself was the living embodiment of that Wisdom. He was and is God's second self, and it is in coming to know God that we discover, individually and in community, how the world really works, what is really worthwhile and what is not, and how to live cheerfully and wisely whether alone or in community. The call of Wisdom, then, is the call of Jesus, the same call as we heard in the Sermon on the Mount: the call to hope and faith, the call to trust God, to put God's kingdom first, the call to abandon worry as a way of life and take up trust instead.

I like to think that Thomas Hatfield would have approved of what we do and say here today. His generosity to the poor and his decisive leadership make him a model, in those respects at least, for the kind of people the world needs today and tomorrow. As Hatfield College goes forward through its second century, it is good to think of it as a community where hope and wisdom can flourish and abound. My congratulations to you on this day, and my prayer for you is that you will be, more and more, a community of this sort.

Even though I am shortly to move to the land whose soldiers were defeated by Bishop Hatfield and his merry men on that day in 1346, I hope that when you reach your second centenary in 2046, you will be winning victories of a different sort: the victory of generosity over greed, the victory of hope over despair, the victory of wisdom over folly, the victory of a happy and outward-looking College community making its unique and distinctive contribution to the life of Durham, of the United Kingdom, and of the wider world.

Appendix Two

DAVID BOARDMAN

Durham Cathedral in Hatfield's Time

Durham Cathedral was built as the shrine of St Cuthbert. When the Saxon Community of St Cuthbert brought their saint's coffin to Durham in 995, they built a white church as a shrine. The Normans began to build the present cathedral in 1093, and when the choir was completed in 1104, Cuthbert's coffin was transferred from the white church to the new shrine which had been prepared for it close to the apse of the cathedral. The transepts were built during the next six years, and the nave was completed in 1133. The apse at the east end, however, became unsafe in the thirteenth century and had to be demolished. It was replaced by the Chapel of the Nine Altars, built in the early English style between 1242 and 1280. The vault of the choir, which had also become unsafe, was rebuilt during the same period. The extension to the east end of the cathedral not only contained more altars for celebrating the Catholic Mass but also provided more space for the great numbers of pilgrims visiting Cuthbert's shrine, which was on a raised platform above the floor of the chapel and was richly decorated with gold, silver, and jewels.

When Thomas Hatfield became Bishop of Durham in 1345, most of the stonework of the Norman cathedral would probably have been in good condition as the building had only been completed in 1133. The east end would have been even newer as it had been rebuilt during the middle of the thirteenth century and finished in 1280. The interior of the church would have been dark, the light filtering through deeply coloured medieval stained-glass windows. There would have been no seating in the nave as it was a space for people to walk, either in procession during services or as groups of pilgrims making their way to the shrine of St Cuthbert. The walls would have been plastered and decorated with colourful paintings and religious icons. A screen separated the people's nave from the choir, which was reserved for the daily worship of the monks in the Benedictine monastery adjoining the south side of the church. The space in the choir was enclosed by stalls and screens, and at the east end was the feretory containing St Cuthbert's shrine, which pilgrims came from all over England to venerate.

Although the cathedral was the seat of the bishopric, attention to affairs of state and administration of a large diocese often limited the extent to which the bishop could be involved in the life of his cathedral. The prior, on the other hand, generally resided in his lodging and thus developed a closer identification with the church where the monks worshipped daily and looked after Cuthbert's shrine. The cathedral community, rather than the bishop, was normally responsible for the maintenance and repair of the building. Bishop Hatfield clearly regarded it as the community's responsibility. After a visitation, he directed the monks in 1355 to repair the defects in the roof of his cathedral church and its bell tower within the space of two years.

Prior John Fossour was elected head of Durham Priory in 1341 and held the position for thirty-three years until he died in 1374. Bishop Hatfield's episcopate was also a long one, beginning in 1345 and lasting thirty-six years until his death in 1381. Fossour had witnessed the battle of Neville's Cross in 1346 and afterwards had written to Hatfield, who was overseas, to tell him about the English victory over the Scots. The more peaceful and prosperous period which followed saw time and money given to enhancing the cathedral and monastery. Four important projects were undertaken between 1366 and 1381: the creation of a shrine to the Venerable Bede in the Galilee Chapel; the installation of the Neville Screen behind the high altar; the construction of the Bishop's Throne and Hatfield Chantry in the choir; and the building of the Great Kitchen in the cloister.

Bede had joined the Saxon community at Wearmouth as a young boy but transferred to the newly founded monastery at Jarrow soon afterwards. He spent the rest of his life there and became the most accomplished scholar of his time, achieving renown as a historian, theologian, scientist, biographer of Cuthbert, and author of commentaries on the Bible. He was buried at Jarrow in 735, but his remains were brought to Durham in 1022 and placed near Cuthbert's tomb in the Saxon white church. When the choir of the cathedral was completed in 1104, Bede's remains were moved close to Cuthbert's shrine. In 1370, however, a separate shrine was created for Bede in the Galilee Chapel, which had been built as an extension to the west end of the cathedral between 1175 and

1189. The chapel's main function was as a Lady chapel, a place where women could gather and celebrate the Mass when the all-male monastic community did not allow women east of the line of black marble laid between the north and south doors of the nave. The Galilee Chapel was also a narthex, or space in which processions began and ended, and from the fourteenth century it served as the bishop's consistory court. The installation of a shrine for the region's greatest scholar symbolized the monastery's growing reputation as a centre of learning and increased the importance of the cathedral as a place of pilgrimage.

The Neville Screen was commissioned by Prior Fossour shortly before he died in 1374. John Neville of Raby Castle contributed most of the cost and almost certainly intended the screen to be an additional monument to his father, Ralph Neville, who was one of the commanders of the English army that had defeated the Scots at the battle of Neville's Cross. Ralph was the first lay person to be buried in the cathedral, initially in a tomb at the front of the nave in 1368 and later in a chantry tomb in the south aisle of the nave. The Neville Screen served not only as a reredos behind the high altar but also as a backdrop to Cuthbert's shrine. The screen was made from stone brought from Caen in Normandy, carved in London in 1376–9, shipped in sections to Newcastle, and transported by road to Durham for reassembly in the cathedral. It is almost certain that Henry Yevele was responsible for the design, which was carved in the Perpendicular style, with five major and four subordinate canopies emphasizing soaring verticality. Doors incorporated into each side of the screen connected the choir to Cuthbert's shrine. There were originally 107 alabaster figures of saints and martyrs in the screen when it was consecrated in 1380, but these were removed during the Reformation. The Neville Screen is an impressive masterpiece of stone carving and is the only surviving medieval canopied reredos in England.[1]

Bishop Hatfield's own legacy to Durham Cathedral is the Bishop's Throne and the Hatfield Chantry below, occupying a bay on the south side of the choir. The great height and length of this extraordinary structure and its elaborate decoration with displays of heraldry were designed to symbolize the power and authority of the Prince-Bishops, who exercised not only spiritual but also political jurisdiction in the palatinate.

1 John Field, *Durham Cathedral: Light of the North* (London, 2006), 87.

When the throne was constructed in 1376–9, it was claimed to be the highest outside Rome. The screen above the gallery at the top of the stairs was carved in the Perpendicular style like its contemporary the Neville Screen, whilst the chantry below reflected the Decorated style. Two carved angels and numerous instances of Hatfield's coat of arms were included in the decoration on each side of the tomb. In earlier centuries bishops had been buried under the floor of the Chapter House. Bishop Antony Bek (1284–311), the first person to be buried in the cathedral, was interred under a simple slab in the Chapel of the Nine Altars, as was Hatfield's predecessor, Bishop Richard Bury (1333–45). Hatfield wanted a chantry tomb bearing his effigy, however, and chose the prominent location below the episcopal throne which he had provided for his successors. He was buried in the tomb in 1381.

Prior Fossour's main legacy to the monastery is the Great Kitchen constructed in the south-west corner of the cloister between 1366 and 1371. The notable master mason John Lewyn of Durham designed this large building, with its unusual octagonal shape and high vault supported by geometrically interlacing stone ribs. The impressive eight-cornered star vault had a central louvre which rendered it virtually fireproof. The kitchen served not only the adjoining refectory in the south range of the cloister but also the prior's lodging further east, and possibly the guest hall and infirmary in the west range (it was centrally located in relation to all of them). The completion of the kitchen would have greatly boosted the morale of the monks and the servants, craftsmen, and tradesmen they employed. When in full use, the kitchen, with its huge fireplaces, ovens, and store cupboards, could provide meals for two hundred to three hundred people every day. The Great Kitchen at Durham has been described as one of the most important surviving monastic buildings in England.[2]

Durham Priory had been founded as a Benedictine monastery by Bishop William of St Calais in 1083, to replace the monastic order of the Community of St Cuthbert on the grounds of alleged laxity. Bishop William summoned to Durham twenty-three monks from the monasteries at Jarrow and Wearmouth to form his fledgling community. The cloister, which was laid out when the building of the church began, was

2 Martin Roberts, *Durham: 1,000 Years of History*, 2nd ed. (Stroud and Charleston, 2003), 81.

the hub of the monastery's daily life and connected its main buildings. Every day the monks assembled in the Chapter House in the east range of the cloister and sat on stone benches set into the walls to hear a reading of a chapter of the Benedictine Rule and conduct monastic business. Seven times a day the monks processed into the choir of the cathedral to attend the divine offices. For the midnight office the monks were awoken from their sleep in the dormitory in the west range of the cloister. During the day-time, when they were not attending divine offices, the monks spent much of their time in the cloister, reading, studying, and teaching, as well as copying manuscripts, music, and liturgical books. The cloister was glazed, and the north range, which contained book cupboards and study carrels, had the advantage of receiving the maximum amount of sunlight. By the fourteenth century the number of monks who met in the Chapter House daily was normally at least sixty and at times approached one hundred. The Black Death, however, brought disaster to the monastic community in 1349. Within a year, fifty-two monks lost their lives, and only forty-six survived.

The Benedictine Rule emphasized the importance of study, and when Bishop William of St Calais founded the monastery, he donated nearly fifty books to the community to encourage the spiritual and intellectual life of its members. He had acquired these books in Normandy as well as in England, and they included a great Bible, service-books, works relating to monastic life, and a copy of Bede's *Ecclesiastical History of the English People*. The monastery's book collection expanded during the twelfth and thirteenth centuries, partly as a result of in-house copying, but mainly because individual members of the community acquired books from outside sources. A surviving fragmentary catalogue from the middle of the fourteenth century indicates that the monastery had two collections of books, one kept in the cloister and the other in the spendement, a strong room off the north-west corner of the cloister. A fully preserved catalogue from the last decade of the fourteenth century shows that there were about five hundred volumes in the cloister and nearly four hundred in the spendement.[3] The cloister collection held volumes in most demand, including Bibles, psalters, and books on theology, history, science, and medicine. The spendement was mainly a store for dupli-

3 Richard Gameson, *Manuscript Treasures of Durham Cathedral* (London, 2010), 17.

cates and less current works. With a total collection of nearly nine hundred volumes – a substantial holding for the time – the priory became the leading institutional library in northern England.

The academic and intellectual life of Durham Priory was strengthened during the fourteenth century by its links with Oxford. Durham had established its own study-cell there in the 1280s to make it easier for its more able monks to obtain a university education. Upon returning to Durham, the monks used their experience and training to further the scholarly work of the monastery and contribute to its growing reputation as "a little university of the north."[4] The stability of the Oxford study-cell, however, was compromised by financial uncertainty for nearly a hundred years. The cell was transformed in 1380 when Bishop Hatfield founded Durham College at Oxford and left a bequest which enabled it to support eight student monks in the study of philosophy and theology and also eight secular students from the priory estates in the study of grammar and theology.

Durham Cathedral's musical tradition was also evolving in the fourteenth century. The Benedictine monks would have sung plainsong in the divine offices from the earliest days of the monastery, but from at least 1345 they received training from a cantor or lay musician who was appointed director of music. Hatfield's predecessor, Bishop Richard Bury, encouraged music in the 1330s and had a clerk who was in charge of the boys of the bishop's chapel. An almonry school which the monastery provided from at least the 1340s gave a basic education to singing boys and poor boys deserving of charitable support. The first singers from the almonry school probably attended Lady masses in the Galilee Chapel. These Lady masses were not part of the monastic offices and therefore provided scope for experimenting with different forms of music. By the 1380s lay clerks were employed to sing polyphony and assist the monks with "trebill song" (three-part harmony). Monastery records from 1414 onwards provide continuous evidence of extensive musical education for boys and monks alike, indicating that boys were singing with the men in some of the divine offices.

During Bishop Hatfield's long episcopate, Durham Cathedral was one of the foremost pilgrimage destinations in England. Active promotion of the pilgrimage ensured that large numbers of pilgrims from all

4 Field, *Durham Cathedral*, 69.

over the country came to visit the shrine of St Cuthbert at the east end of the cathedral and, after 1370, the shrine of the Venerable Bede at the west end. Hatfield made his mark on the cathedral by installing the huge Bishop's Throne in the choir and left visitors with no doubt about the power and authority of the Prince-Bishops. At the same time, by founding Durham College at Oxford in 1380 and leaving it a bequest, Hatfield showed his recognition of the importance of a university education for the monks who had established Durham's reputation as a centre of learning and scholarship.

Bibliography

Dufferwiel, Martin. *Durham: Over 1,000 Years of History and Legend.* 1996; repr. Edinburgh: Mainstream, 2004.

Field, John. *Durham Cathedral: Light of the North.* London: Third Millennium Publishing, 2006.

Gameson, Richard. *Manuscript Treasures of Durham Cathedral.* London: Third Millennium Publishing, 2010.

Pocock, Douglas, ed. *St Cuthbert and Durham Cathedral: A Celebration.* 2nd rev. ed. Durham: City of Durham Trust, 1995.

Roberts, Martin. *Durham: 1,000 Years of History.* 2nd ed. Stroud and Charleston: Tempus Publishing, 2003.

Contributors

Anthony Bash is Chaplain of Hatfield College, Tutor for Postgraduates at Hatfield College, and Honorary Research Fellow in the Department of Theology and Religion, Durham University. He has published on biblical studies, ethics and canon law, and, most recently, is the author of *Forgiveness and Christian Ethics* (2007) and *Just Forgiveness* (2011).

David Boardman has served as a Hatfield College Tutor and as a Durham Cathedral Guide. He was previously Senior Lecturer in Education at the University of Birmingham and has published extensively in the field of geographical education.

Richard H. Britnell is Emeritus Professor of History at Durham University. He writes mainly about the social and economic history of Britain in the eleventh to sixteenth centuries. Professor Britnell taught at Durham University from 1966 until his retirement in 2003. He is joint editor of the Surtees Society, founded in 1834, which has published over two hundred volumes of records relating to the history of northern England, including William Greenwell's edition of *Bishop Hatfield's Survey* (first printed in 1857, reprinted in 1967). He was elected a Fellow of the British Academy in 2005.

Tim Burt is the fifteenth Master of Hatfield College and Professor of Geography at Durham University. Previously, he was a Lecturer at Oxford University and a Fellow of Keble College. He has published extensively in the fields of hydrology, geomorphology, and climatology.

Christian D. Liddy is Senior Lecturer in the Department of History at Durham. He is the author of two books: *War, Politics and Finance in Late Medieval English Towns: Bristol, York and the Crown, 1350–1400* (2005) and *The Bishopric of Durham in the Late Middle Ages: Lordship, Community and the Cult of St Cuthbert* (2008). He is also the co-editor of *North-East England in the Later Middle Ages* (2005).

W. Mark Ormrod is Professor of History at the University of York, where he has served as Director of the Centre for Medieval Studies, Head of the Department of History, and Academic Coordinator for Arts and Humanities. He has published extensively on the political, administrative, social, and cultural history of the later Middle Ages, including *Political Life in Medieval England* (1995), *The Evolution of English Justice* (with Anthony Musson, 1999), and *A Social History of England, 1200–1500* (with Rosemary Horrox, 2006). His new biography of Edward III, published in 2011, appears in Yale University Press's English Monarchs series.

Michael Prestwich is Emeritus Professor of History at Durham University, having retired in 2008. He was a Pro-Vice-Chancellor from 1992 to 1999. The books he has written include *War, Politics and Finance under Edward I* (1972), *The Three Edwards* (1980), *Edward I* (1988), *Plantagenet England, 1225–1360* (2005), and, most recently, *Knight* (2010). He received an OBE in 2010.

N.T. Wright served as Bishop of Durham from 2003 to 2010 and is currently Research Professor of New Testament and Early Christianity at the University of St Andrews. He is among the foremost New Testament scholars in the world and the author of numerous books, including *Scripture and the Authority of God* (2005, revised in 2011), *The Challenge of Jesus* (1999, revised in 2011), and, most recently, *How God Became King: The Forgotten Story of the Gospels* (2012).

Index